THE ESCAPE

THE

ESCAPE;

OR,

A LEAP FOR FREEDOM.

A Drama

IN FIVE ACTS.

———•◦•———

BY WILLIAM WELLS BROWN.

EDITED, WITH AN INTRODUCTION BY, JOHN ERNEST.

———•◦•———

THE UNIVERSITY OF TENNESSEE PRESS
Knoxville

The paper used in this book meets the minimum requirements
of ANSI/NISO Z39.48-1992 (R 1997) (Permanence of Paper). The binding
materials have been chosen for strength and durability.

Library of Congress Cataloging-in-Publication Data

Brown, William Wells, 1815–1884.
The escape, or, A leap for freedom: a drama in five acts / by William
Wells Brown; edited, with an introduction by, John Ernest.—1st ed.
    p. cm.
Includes bibliographical references (p.   ).
ISBN 1-57233-105-4 (cl.: alk. paper) — ISBN 1-57233-106-2 (pbk.: alk.paper)
1. Abolitionists—Drama. 2. Afro-Americans—Drama. 3. Slaveholders—Drama.
4. Missouri—Drama. 5. Slavery—Drama. 6. Slaves—Drama. I. Title: Escape.
II. Title: Leap for freedom. III. Ernest, John. IV. Title.
PS1139.B9 E8 2000
812'.4—dc21   00-009484

CONTENTS

———•—•—

ACKNOWLEDGMENTS

I am grateful to Doug Lanier and Rebecca Mays Ernest for their help in preparing this text. I am indebted to William L. Andrews, Edward Baptist, Russ Castronovo, Stanley Harrold, and Jeff Kerr-Ritchie, who carefully read early plans for this project and suggested improvements. I owe an even greater debt to Russ Castronovo and especially John Grammer and Stanley Harrold for their careful readings of the introduction and detailed suggestions for improving it. Peter A. Dorsey offered detailed and wise advice on my essay on Brown's play that led to this edition, and I am grateful to him for helping me to bring my scattered thoughts into focus. I am indebted as well to Mavis Bryant for her copyediting skills, and to Stan Ivester for his careful attention to the integrity of Brown's text and to the intentions of my own. Finally, any expression of gratitude seems an inadequate response to the hard work of Joyce Harrison, who suggested this project in the first place and guided me through its many stages.

INTRODUCTION

In 1856, the well-known African American writer and abolitionist
William Wells Brown introduced something new to the antislavery lecture circuit: a dramatic reading of an original drama, *Experience; or, How
to Give the Northern Man a Backbone*.[1] The play was never published,
though numerous reviews appeared in the antislavery press, and an over-
view of the play appeared in the National Anti-Slavery Standard. According to these sources, Brown offered in Experience a satirical response to
a book by a white northerner, the Reverend Dr. Nehemiah Adams's *A
South-Side View of Slavery; or, Three Months at the South*, published in
1854. In that book, Adams reports that his journey in the South has led
him to revise his impressions of slavery. Accordingly, he counsels his white
northern readers to hold to racially grounded ideals of national union
and "Christian" patience: "Let us feel and act fraternally with regard to
the South, defend them against interference, abstain from every thing
assuming and dictatorial, leave them to manage their institution in view
of their accountability to God . . . and we may expect that American slavery will cease to be any thing but a means of good to the African race."[2]
Brown's play, in response, concerns a northern minister ("a Boston D.D."
named Jeremiah Adderson) and author of a "South-side View of Slavery"
who embarks on a tour through the South. "By a strange turn of events," as
one summary has it, "the pastor is sold into slavery."[3] As might be expected,
the pastor, now having first-hand experience of slavery, soon revises his
former opinions. The play ends appropriately with an "eloquent appeal"
by a fugitive slave and a "Grand Poetic Finale," in which, one can only
imagine, the point is brought back home to the North.[4]

As Brown's biographer, William Edward Farrison, has noted, this play
was one of Brown's many attempts to vary the form of his antislavery

message in an effort to "win and hold the attention of possible converts."[5] As Brown himself noted, he could make more money for the cause at these events if he were to read a play than if he delivered a lecture. In fact, the plays were so well received that in 1856 the *Liberator* announced that Brown had "given up his agency" with the American Anti-Slavery Society to "devote his time to giving his lyceum lectures and the reading of his drama." The plays were not staged or performed; Brown simply read all the parts himself, "with a most happy dramatic effect," as one reviewer noted.[6]

By this time, Brown already had moved well beyond mid-nineteenth-century literary expectations for an African American writer. By the mid-1850s, Brown had edited a collection of songs, and he had published fiction, two editions of a travel narrative, a lecture on "St. Domingo: Its Revolutions and Its Patriots," and various editions of his well-known *Narrative of William W. Brown, A Fugitive Slave, Written by Himself* (1847). Thus it is not surprising that Brown would turn to drama. More-over, at a time when blackface minstrelsy was both widely popular and deeply influential, Brown might have seen a certain poetic justice in placing a humbled white northerner in the midst of what one advertise-ment identified as a "laughable and highly interesting" drama.

While we can only speculate about Brown's first play, we can still read the text of another drama Brown wrote as he launched his new career as an antislavery playwright. *The Escape; or, A Leap for Freedom* (1858) was the first published play by an African American writer.[7] *The Escape* is important beyond its status as the beginning of a literary tradi-tion, however. In this work, Brown explores the complexities of United States culture in the late 1850s, an era when tensions between the North and the South were threatening to explode into civil war. As Brown knew, these sectional battles rarely attended to the conditions of those of Afri-can descent who were enslaved in the South and denied basic civil rights in the North. Nehemiah Adams, the primary target of Brown's first play, exemplifies the flexible ethical views of white northerners who spoke of national unity as if it were of concern only to white men. In that play, Brown satirizes the white minister's smug assurance of intellectual superiority and moral certainty. Brown's character Jeremiah Adderson discovers that he has something to learn about slavery, and that therefore he has some-thing to learn, too, about the issues upon which he once held forth with such certainty.

The Escape is arguably an extension of the theme of his first effort, for in many ways Brown is still looking to "give a northern man a backbone." In this case, however, the northern man is not the identifiable Nehemiah Adams but the generic "Mr. White," a northerner who is attacked in the

South for his views on slavery and who responds to this attack by hiding and returning to the safety of the North. Like the earlier Dr. Adderson, Mr. White has a lot to learn about the ways in which his world and his very identity have been shaped by the system of slavery, seemingly so distant in the South. And Brown is only too happy to supply the lessons, exploring everything from the sexual violence so common in the South to poverty in the North, from timid white antislavery advocates to bold and inventive slaves, from the Underground Railroad to the secrets of the theoretically sacred realm of white domestic relations. This is a drama played out on the national stage, and Brown seems to have chosen his cast of characters carefully, so as to expose the cultural fictions so fundamental to white identity and national unity.

Entirely familiar with the expectations of white audiences, even those who gathered to hear an antislavery message, Brown was very much interested in the literary conventions and racial assumptions that shaped American history and culture. In the mid-1850s, it certainly was an innovation for a black antislavery lecturer to read an original drama. Yet, in itself, the five-act play that Brown wrote and read offered very little material that was new. *The Escape* is, in part, a recontextualization and a significant rearrangement of established literary conventions and familiar antislavery commentary. The play's six principal characters are all, as Farrison has observed, "stock characters":[8] Dr. and Mrs. Gaines, the white slaveholders and owners of the farm at Muddy Creek, Missouri; Glen and Melinda, both enslaved, who are in love but forbidden to marry; Mr. White, the white northerner who visits the South and confronts the realities of slavery; and Cato, house servant to the Gaineses and Dr. Gaines's recently trained medical assistant. Dr. and Mrs. Gaines are duplicitous and morally bankrupt slaveholders, and much of the plot has to do with Dr. Gaines's attempts to make Melinda his mistress (as he has succeeded in doing with others, the play suggests). Through the farce of the Gaineses' marriage and the violent disregard for humanity that underlies their professions of religious faith, we see the effects of slavery on the character of the enslavers.

In this play, too, we see a broad range of responses to the system of slavery. Glen and Melinda, a sentimental couple separated by injustice, melodramatically give voice to ethereal ideals of love and to holy destinies obstructed by a corrupt social system. Mr. White, a white northerner who considers himself devoted to the antislavery cause, expresses that devotion in sentimental talk more than in action. Cato is a figure straight out of blackface minstrelsy. He dresses in what clearly is intended as a comical imitation of white fashion; he pulls the wrong tooth of a slave with a toothache; and at the end of the play, when he assigns himself a new name—the Reverend Alexander Washington Napoleon Pompey Cæsar—to suit his anticipated dignity as a freeman, he praises it not as respectable but as "suspectable." The various principal characters, as well as the various plot lines, all are united when Melinda and Glen, secretly having married, escape to the North, precipitating the dramatic concluding confrontation at Niagara Falls, "the kind of incident which had become a part of the stock of antislavery literature."[9] As the various parts of the play come together, so does Brown's commentary on slavery, not as a simple moral issue to be debated but as a cultural system touching the lives of all involved. And, as Brown argued throughout his career, all Americans were involved.

No Escape: Slavery, Race, and American Culture

The development of the system of slavery from the American Revolution to the Civil War was complexly intertwined with the formation and development of the United States. Slavery was even, as historian Edmund S. Morgan has argued, central to the concept of liberty celebrated as the bedrock of the nation.[10] The country's founders were not blind to the contradiction inherent in staging a revolution in the cause of liberty and then forming a nation that included slavery. Nor were the enslaved, who filed petitions with various state legislators arguing for their right to freedom by drawing on the ideological rhetoric that had powered the Revolutionary War—an argument that had particular force since many African Americans had fought in that war. Thomas Jefferson had given slavery a prominent place in the Declaration of Independence, listing it among the evils which had been forced upon the colonies and consequently justified revolution against the British crown. Jefferson, in his reflections on the character of the new nation, *Notes on the State of Virginia*, famously worried about the moral consequences of the nation's reliance on the system of slavery:

> Can the liberties of a nation be thought secure when we have removed their only firm basis, a conviction in the minds of the people that these liberties are the gift of God? That they are not to be violated but with his wrath? Indeed I tremble for my country when I reflect that God is just: that his justice cannot sleep for ever: that considering numbers, nature and natural means only, a revolution of the wheel of fortune, an exchange of situation, is among possible events: that it may become probable by supernatural interference![11]

Jefferson was not alone in such musings. Indeed, many northern states (with economies less reliant on slavery) abolished slavery—though in most cases providing only for gradual abolition—in the decades following the American Revolution. But economic arguments prevailed, particularly after the invention of the cotton gin in 1793. The cotton gin contributed to the expansion of the system of slavery in the South and made that region increasingly dependent upon slave labor. In 1790, the slave population in the United States was under 700,000; by 1860, the enslaved population totaled nearly four million.[12] In 1808, the Atlantic slave trade legally ended, though for decades people continued to be stolen into slavery from Africa and transported to the United States illegally. The domestic slave trade (trade within and between the states of the Union) remained legal and assumed growing economic importance in the South.

Through economic and political ties, slavery was a presence in the North, too—sufficiently so that some commentators chastised northerners for speaking against slavery while implicitly supporting it in the marketplace. Consider, for example, the argument presented by David Christy in his 1855 book *Cotton Is King*, in which Christy presented slavery as a firmly entrenched problem, one which could not be limited to or blamed on the South, an argument that southerners quickly applied to the defense of slavery. Christy asserted, with sound logic, that it was virtually impossible for northerners with money not to be, in some ways, the beneficiaries of slavery. The economic system that depended heavily upon slavery, Christy noted, reached far beyond the South; many in the North who attacked slavery still profited by it, if only in indirect ways. Accordingly, Christy argued,

> in speaking of the economical connections of slavery, with the other material interests of the world, we have called it a *tri-partite alliance*. It is more than this. It is *quadruple*. Its structure includes four parties, arranged thus: The Western Agriculturalists; the Southern Planters; the English Manufacturers; and the American Abolitionists! By this arrangement, the Abolitionists do not stand in direct contact with slavery; they imagine, therefore, that they have clean hands and pure hearts, so far as sustaining the system is concerned. But they, no less than their allies, aid in promoting the interests of slavery.[13]

Christy was deliberately provocative in involving "American Abolitionists" in this argument, although many antislavery sympathizers tried mightily to avoid supporting slavery in any way.[14] But, despite the efforts of abolitionists to avoid economic involvement in slavery, Christy's argument was influential. Indeed, arguments like Christy's understandably left many northern antislavery advocates groping for a response, defensive about their presumptive moral advantage in this debate.

As slavery developed in the South, it increasingly became a central focus of sectional tensions played out in the halls of Congress and in the pages of numerous books and periodicals. What I am calling "tensions" between the North and South were more than just ideological skirmishes between groups of people who either defended or attacked the system of slavery. The battles over slavery were rarely as neat or as simple as twentieth-century readers often make them out to be. At the nation's beginning, many southerners as well as many northerners followed Jefferson in worrying about the moral implications of slavery, while at the same time supporting it either economically or politically. The ideological contradictions of a nation devoted both to the cause of liberty and to the system of slavery could not be ignored; they had to be accounted for in any attempt to define national identity.

Such attempts were many. Much of New England writing, for example, was devoted to defining what was particular, unique, and even superior (as New England writers saw it) about New England. Increasingly, many New Englanders relied for contrast upon an image of the South as the home of both slavery and the licentiousness that accompanied slavery.[15] Southerners, in turn, relied on contrasts with the North to define the South. John Grammer, a historian of southern literature and culture, has explored the struggle by southerners to define the South, noting that, "as it became clear in the 1830s that slavery was a permanent feature rather than a temporary blemish on the southern landscape, southerners were increasingly compelled to contemplate the conflict between their intellectual legacy and their present social order."[16] Many northerners felt similarly compelled, for the defense of slavery was not entirely a southern project. As historian Larry E. Tise has written, "The popular notion is that proslavery was a pursuit unique to southern slaveholding Americans. A composite biographical study of nearly three hundred individuals who published defenses of slavery in the United States suggests that the pursuit was almost without geographical distinction."[17] Virtually every area of American culture was involved in the defense and maintenance of slavery. Arguments over slavery involved every level of government and law, shaped scientific theory and practices, penetrated virtually all areas of economic exchange, guided theology and the governance of religious institutions, influenced conceptions of gender, defined ideologies of race, and provided materials to those who worked to define regional and national identity in opposition to other regions and nations.

These sectional divisions led to ideological battles that at times were grounded only loosely in fact but nevertheless were powerful in their effects. Some of the most prominent defenders of slavery, for example, attempted to change the direction of these battles by attacking industrialism in the northern United States and in Britain. These writers contrasted slavery with what they characterized as the heartless methods of the northern capitalists, although many historians have argued that southern plantation slavery itself was a capitalist system.[18] If those who took this line of defense had no leg to stand on in their presentation of slavery as a benevolent system, their attacks on the poverty and oppression fostered by industry had considerable force. Some of the most prominent proslavery commentators took this argument to the extreme, drawing on the socialist theory of the time. Edmund Ruffin, for example, suggested that socialist theorists were largely right in their assessment of social ills and theoretical solutions but were mistaken as to the best method of achieving a sound approach to the management of labor. "Our system of domestic slavery offers in use," Ruffin argued in 1853, "and to the greatest profit for all parties in the association, the realization of all that is sound and valuable in the socialists' theories and doctrines."[19] Henry Hughes, in his *A Treatise on Sociology, Theoretical and Practical* (1854), agreed. Similarly, George Fitzhugh, one of the most ardent promoters of this argument, vigorously presented slavery as superior to capitalism ("the White Slave Trade") in his books, *Sociology for the South; or, The Failure of Free Society* (1854) and *Cannibals All! Or, Slaves Without Masters* (1857). Capitalists, Fitzhugh argued, used labor without care for the laborers; slaveholders, he said, had to care for the laborers, providing slaves with "food, raiment, house, fuel, and everything else necessary to the physical well-being of himself and family."[20]

Many northern readers naturally would distrust Fitzhugh's description of the South's treatment of the enslaved; and many readers would recognize that he failed completely to address the issue of ownership of people and the "social death" that sociologist Orlando Patterson identifies as one of the central features of slavery.[21] But arguments like these were not easily dismissed; as misleading as they were in their representations of slavery, they were largely correct in their representations of the laboring classes in the growing industrial systems of the North and England. In the years before the Civil War, most African American writers and intellectuals felt compelled to respond to these arguments.[22] Indeed, William Wells Brown encountered just this argument (among many others) in the target of his original play, Adams's *A South-Side View of Slavery*. In this work, Adams adapts the northern response to poverty—paternalistic charity, benevolent disregard—to the defense of slavery: "As Charles Lamb tells us not to inquire too narrowly of every mendicant whether the 'wife and six young children' are a fiction, but to give, and enjoy it, so there was a temptation to disregard for the time the idea of slavery, and, becoming a mere utilitarian, to think of three millions of our population as being under perfect control, and in this instance indisputably to their benefit."[23] As Adams here suggests, comparisons of capitalist labor and American slavery made it possible to arrive at a kind of ideological stalemate, in which the poor and the enslaved alike were viewed simply as bad off and in need of the benevolent feelings and charity of the privileged classes.

In short, the consideration of slavery as an approach to the management of labor provided not only convenient proslavery defenses against abolitionists but also, in the North, powerful rhetorical tools for the organization of labor within a developing capitalist economy. David R. Roediger has demonstrated that slavery in the United States shaped the development of an antebellum labor movement that was not only "exceptional in its rhetoric" but also "exceptionally militant as it critiqued evolving capitalist social relations as a kind of slavery." By use of the vague and inclusive phrase *white slavery*, "abolitionists, free blacks, bankers, factory owners and prison labor could, in sundry combinations, be cast as villains in a loose plot to enslave white workers." Although the comparison between white hireling and black slave could encourage analyses of wage labor as bondage, the emphasis on visible social contrasts "also could reassure wage workers that they belonged to the ranks of 'free white labor'" and highlight the need for progress toward improved labor conditions for white workers. In short, Roediger argues, "the growing popular sense of whiteness represented a hesitantly emerging consensus holding together a very diverse white working class" by enabling white antebellum workers to "displace anxieties within the white population onto blacks."[24] As Frederick Douglass put it in 1855, "The impression is cunningly made, that slavery is the only power that can prevent the laboring white man from falling to the level of the slave's poverty and degradation."[25]

As these comments on labor suggest, one of the many effects of the system of slavery was an increasingly developed ideology of race, a conception of race that could mark *black* and *white* as fundamentally different realms of life with inherently different possibilities and degrees of potential. The development of an ideology of white supremacy—built, as it was, on an unstable foundation—was used increasingly after the 1830s to justify slavery in the South, while also supporting and promoting racism in the North. Black abolitionists especially emphasized that the struggle against racism was an essential part of the struggle against slavery—for, indeed, many black abolitionists experienced prejudice even in the anti-slavery movement. Many African Americans who traveled to Europe emphasized how different their experience there was compared to life in the northern United States—experience ranging from public transportation and hotel accommodations to personal interactions at all levels of society. Virtually all African American antislavery activists made racial prejudice a regular and prominent theme of their lectures and publications, and many were active in the struggle against racism. Sojourner Truth, Frances Ellen Watkins Harper, William Still, and others protested discrimination in public transportation; in Boston, William C. Nell and others fought against segregation and discrimination in the school system. Among the most powerful of the many writers who denounced racism was Frederick Douglass. In an editorial entitled "Prejudice Against Color," published in his paper *The North Star* (13 June 1850), Douglass argued that, "properly speaking, *prejudice against color* does not exist in this country. The feeling (or whatever it is) which we call *prejudice*, is no less than a *murderous, hell-born hatred* of every virtue which may adorn the character of a *black man*."[26] Racism was always a presence in northern life and at times could explode into a more immediate threat. In 1829, for example, there were antiblack riots in Cincinnati, and similar riots occurred in Philadelphia and New York in 1834.

If this violent insistence upon racial difference suggests that many white people were insecure about what whiteness actually meant, that is because the very concept of race was, as is recognized today, a social fiction. Moreover, it was a fiction increasingly exposed by the blurring of racial lines brought about by sexual contact (often forced) between black and white Americans. Sexual violence stood at the core of slavery, and, as race came to be considered the foundation for the slave system, American culture increasingly was characterized by what cultural scholar Karen Sánchez-Eppler has termed a "fascination with miscegenation."[27] Policing racial lines was one of the central concerns of many white writers. Consider, for example, the words of John Campbell, published in his feverish book-length tirade against the notion of social equality for African Americans, entitled *Negro-Mania: Being an Examination of the Falsely Assumed Equality of the Various Races of Men* (1851). "Time nor circumstance nor climate affect not the negro race," according to Campbell; "all nature forbids an amalgamation between them and the Caucasians. Nature tolerates not hybrids, or mules, or mulattoes. It is clearly proven that a race between the three typical stocks, can only be maintained by a continual drain upon a parent stock."[28] Apparently, though, all nature did not forbid such amalgamations, for mixed-race American-born men and women were in fact numerous. As the African American clergyman and abolitionist Henry Highland Garnet argued in 1848, "Skillful men have set themselves to work at analyzation, and yet in many cases they are perplexed in deciding where to draw the line between the Negro and the Anglo-Saxon." Noting that the crossing of this line was a "stubborn fact" of life in the United States, Garnet asserted that "this western world is destined to be filled with a mixed race." He argued that, if Americans of color were forcibly relocated elsewhere, included in the exodus would be a number of prominent "white" Americans.[29]

Antislavery writers, black and white, emphasized again and again both the sexual violence common under slavery and the effect of that violence in producing people whose mixed-race status challenged a social order based on deliberate separation of the races. William Wells Brown, for example, centered his 1853 novel, *Clotel; or, The President's Daughter*, on rumors that Jefferson had fathered a child with one of his slaves. Brown began the first chapter of that novel with a reminder that such practices were common: "With the growing population of slaves in the Southern States of America, there is a fearful increase of half whites, most of whose fathers are slaveowners, and their mothers slaves. . . . In all the cities and towns of the slave states, the real Negro, or clear black, does not amount to more than one in every four of the slave population. This fact is, of itself, the best evidence of the degraded and immoral condition of the relation of master and slave in the United States of America."[30] While Brown was no social scientist, he was able to buttress his general point with statements from the white statesmen Henry Clay and John Randolph, from personal experience, and from the evidence of appearances. Another fugitive slave author, Harriet Jacobs, agreed. In her autobiographical narrative, *Incidents in the Life of a Slave Girl* (1861), she emphasized:

> No pen can give an adequate description of the all-pervading corruption produced by slavery. The slave girl is reared in an atmosphere of licentiousness and fear. The lash and the foul talk of her master and his sons are her teachers. When she is fourteen or fifteen, her owner, or his sons, or the overseer, or perhaps all of them, begin to bribe her with presents. If these fail to accomplish their purpose, she is whipped or starved into submission to their will. She may have had religious principles inculcated by some pious mother or grandmother, or some good mistress; she may have a lover, whose good opinion and peace

of mind are dear to her heart; or the profligate men who have power over her may be exceedingly odious to her. But resistance is hopeless.[31]

Brown portrays just such an attempt at resistance in *The Escape*; and in *Clotel*, he examines the effects of the intermixing of the races, telling stories of slaves who could pass for white and of white people kidnapped and sold into slavery.

RESISTANCE AND IDENTITY: RACE, GENDER, AND SLAVERY

As Harriet Jacobs's description of the "all-pervading corruption produced by slavery" suggests, the struggle for freedom, or even the struggle for survival, was fundamentally a struggle of identity, one in which one's gender inevitably played a major role. Jacobs, like the character Melinda in *The Escape*, was the object of her owner's lust. From a young age, she found herself resisting the attempts of her owner to corrupt her so as to seduce her, as if he were determined to possess the will, as well as the body, of the enslaved girl. Like Dr. Gaines with Melinda in *The Escape*, the slaveholder in *Incidents* offers to "make a lady" of the young Linda Brent (the name Jacobs assumes in her narrative) by building a cottage in a secluded area where he plans to keep her as his mistress.[32] In *Incidents*, which surveys the many forms of sexual violence under slavery, Jacobs asserts that a young enslaved girl "will become prematurely knowing in evil things. Soon she will learn to tremble when she hears her master's footfall. She will be compelled to realize that she is no longer a child. If God has bestowed beauty upon her, it will prove her greatest curse. That which commands admiration in the white woman only hastens the degradation of the female slave."[33] In *The Escape*, Brown emphasizes the vulnerability and degradation of female slaves by involving marriage in this story of enslavement. Glen wins the affections of a woman whose will Dr. Gaines has not succeeded in bending to his own; and Glen makes of that woman, Melinda, a *wife*. In this way, Glen challenges the quiet double standard by which Dr. Gaines might have justified, if only to himself, his lecherous intent. As Dr. Gaines becomes even more determined to have his way, Melinda responds in kind by insisting upon the integrity of her own cultural role as woman and wife. "Bid me do anything else," Melinda tells Dr. Gaines, for the first time revealing her secret marriage to Glen, "but I beseech you not to commit a double crime,—outrage a woman, and make her false to her husband."

Melinda's story is one often told in the pages of antislavery literature—so often, in fact, that Melinda is an identifiable character type, the "tragic mulatta" (a corresponding male type is the "tragic mulatto"). In color and manners, this character usually is indistinguishable from white (usually middle- or upper-class) people. In some cases, as in Frances E. W. Harper's novel *Iola Leroy* (1892), the tragic mulatta grows up believing she is white. In this way the character draws attention to the permeability of the "color line" in American culture, and beyond that to the permeability of cultural categories of racial identities. This is certainly Brown's point in *The Escape*, for example, when Major Moore visits the Gaines residence and mistakenly assumes that one of the slaves is the child of Dr. and Mrs. Gaines. "Madam," he says to Mrs. Gaines, "I should have known that this was the Colonel's son, if I had met him in California; for he looks so much like his papa." Brown again emphasizes this point when the slave trader, Mr. Walker, confidentially assumes that the slave sold by Mr. Wildmarsh is Wildmarsh's own daughter. "You need not be ashamed to own it to me," Walker notes, "for I am mum upon such matters." In other literary works, where the person of mixed race grows up ignorant of what the culture would term her or his "true" heritage (that is, the "drop of black blood" by which the color line increasingly was defined), the cultural fictions of race lead to the "tragedy" of the mulatta's identity, once that identity is discovered or revealed. In Harper's novel, Iola Leroy is sold into slavery upon her father's death, a plot line that William Wells Brown had explored earlier in his novel *Clotel*.

The tragic mulatta character emphasizes the extent to which concepts of gender in antebellum American culture were linked to concepts of race and shaped by the legal and social demands of the system of slavery. Antislavery literature both responded to and reflected slavery's inevitable corruption of gender roles. As Paul Gilmore has argued, "Antislavery rhetoric consistently spoke of the debilitating effects of slavery in gendered terms. During the antebellum period, rising bourgeois ideologies of the family foregrounded gender—as defined by strictly distinguished traits—as an essential quality of humanity. Being human meant being either a 'true woman' or a 'real man.'"[34] Slavery made it impossible for a woman to perform the role of a "true woman," in the terms defined by white nineteenth-century culture, for enslaved women had little control over their ability to defend their virtue, create a home, attend to their families' physical and spiritual health, or nurture or protect their children.[35] Similarly, male slaves had little opportunity to perform the culturally defined role of a "real man," for they could not protect their wives and children, and they had no control over the economic, physical, or even geographical security of their families.

As Gilmore notes, "Abolitionists faced two primary problems in representing black manhood: first, slavery was constructed as antithetical to ideal manhood; second, because ideas of enslavement were intrinsic to the construction of blackness, blackness itself came to be seen as unmanly."[36] This challenge to masculine identity is at the center of much of Brown's work. In his *Narrative of William W. Brown, A Fugitive Slave* (1847), for example, Brown tells of hearing his mother's cries as she is whipped but being able to do nothing to assist her. Brown retold that story often, and other men who survived slavery to tell their stories likewise emphasized the helplessness they felt in trying to fulfill their roles as men.

Particularly for women under slavery, the effect of the system of slavery was to deny the authority of gender while simultaneously exploiting the gender of the enslaved. In *The Escape*, as I have noted, Brown emphasizes the situation of women under slavery when he has Melinda beg Dr. Gaines not to "commit a double crime" against her. The ideologies of race and the system of slavery, though, undermine Melinda's status as both woman and wife. Slave marriages had only tenuous validity and could be broken up by sale or at the whim of the slaveholder; and women were subject to outrages against which they had almost no recourse. As Hazel V. Carby has noted with regard to Jacobs's *Incidents*, at the end of her narrative Linda Brent remains "excluded from the domain of the home, the sphere within which womanhood and motherhood were defined. Without a 'woman's sphere,' both were rendered meaningless."[37] Black women were assigned a separate sphere, and their social roles were limited to what one historian has labeled the "Jezebel" and the "Mammy." The Jezebel stereotype of black female identity was based upon the assumption that "black women were exceptionally sensual"; the "Mammy" stereotype was based upon the domestic position of black women, who were expected to be "completely dedicated to the white family, especially to the children of that family."[38] Beyond the situation of women who were victims of either a slaveholder's lecherous intent or the white family's condescending dependence was the fact that such concepts as womanhood and motherhood were barely recognized beyond the near-inevitability of producing children who would inherit the condition of the mother. For example, in *Narrative of the Life of Frederick Douglass, an American Slave*, Douglass tells the story of a poor slaveowner who, looking to increase his holdings, purchases a woman to serve as a "breeder." "After buying her," Douglass reports, "[Covey] hired a married man . . . to live with him one year; and him he used to fasten up with her every night! The result was, that, at the end of the year, the miserable woman gave birth to twins."[39] Joanne M. Braxton's term for female slaves thus "degraded and dehumanized" is the "outraged mother": "She is a mother because motherhood was virtually unavoidable under slavery; she is outraged because of the intimacy of her oppression."[40]

It is hardly surprising, then, that white mothers would respond particularly to the multiple violations of womanhood common under slavery. In 1837, for example, at the Anti-Slavery Convention of American Women, Mrs. A. L. Cox put forth a resolution proclaiming, "There is no class of women to whom the anti-slavery cause makes so direct and powerful an appeal as to *mothers*."[41] At that time and throughout the period of antislavery efforts, many women agreed. Many white women found, too, that slavery was an increasingly intimate presence in their own lives. Many nineteenth-century readers were familiar with stories of the outrages committed under slavery; but, as Brown and other writers emphasized, the gendered violence of slavery extended beyond black men and women. Consider, for example, Jacobs's account of a "young lady" who inherits both a fortune and seven slaves, a mother and her six children. Jacobs presents her as one of the conspicuous exceptions to the rule of cruelty, one for whom "religion was not a garb put on for Sunday," as "there was some reality in her religion." Caught in the contradictions of the system, the lady tries to act according to her beliefs and attempts to teach those beliefs to others by example as well as word. However, she falls victim to love, marrying a man who is interested in her wealth. Before her marriage, she offers to manumit her slaves, "telling them that her marriage might make unexpected changes in their destiny," but the enslaved family does not know enough of the world of slavery to seize the opportunity. When her new husband assumes control of the slaves, who had "never felt slavery" but now were "convinced of its reality," the lady can only admit to the "free" patriarch of the enslaved family, "I no longer have the power I had a week ago." Power lost by marriage, including the power to act upon one's moral beliefs, was, of course, a prominent concern of the feminist abolitionists who drew upon the rhetoric of enslavement. The sequel of this story is that the husband produces a child with one of the slaves, and the young lady is forced to recognize that "her own husband had violated the purity she had so carefully inculcated." The husband's image is to be seen clearly in the face of the enslaved child, making obvious the unspoken bonds that characterize slavery's "invisible" community, the unacknowledged presence of the enslavers among the enslaved.[42] When one reads this story at its various levels, one can understand why the antislavery movement proved to be so important to the organization and ideology of the white women's movement. As historian Jacqueline Jones has argued, "The system of bondage ultimately involved the subordination of all women, both black and white, to masters-husbands whose behavior ranged from benevolent to tyrannical, but always within a patriarchal context."[43]

In many of his publications, Brown emphasizes the multifarious violations either sanctioned by, or inevitable under, the system of slavery. His commentary on the institution of marriage is particularly forceful, for marriage was Brown's standard symbol of cultural stability. Claudia Tate has demonstrated the extent to which African Americans of the nineteenth century viewed marriage "as central to their personal advancement, as central to the prosperity of their families and communities, indeed as central to the progress of civilization itself."[44] Working in a similar vein, Ann duCille has noted that the literary tradition of the African American "marriage plot," in which the cultural and political significance of marriage is promoted, began with Brown's *Clotel*. In that novel, Brown asserts that marriage is "the first and most important institution of human existence—the foundation of all civilization and culture—the root of church and state." Marriage is, the narrator of *Clotel* further asserts, "the most intimate covenant of heart formed among mankind; and for many persons the only relation in which they feel the true sentiments of humanity."[45] In *The Escape*, the corruption of marriage is amply represented by Dr. and Mrs. Gaines, whose relationship is characterized by distrust and deception, and who together base their fortunes on the misfortunes of others, looking to "Providence" to "send some disease among us for our benefit" (36). As the Gaines marriage suggests, "the true sentiments of humanity" are distant from the lives of the white characters in *The Escape*.

As goes marriage, so goes "the root of church and state." Mrs. Gaines talks about "religious experience" with Rev. John Pinchen, a traveling clergyman, all the time turning to Hannah to promise, "I'll whip you well." Pinchen himself purchases slaves to cover traveling expenses as his tour of religious visits continues. Mr. Wildmarsh plans to sell his unacknowledged daughter. Southern slaveholders denounce the Constitution. Brown dramatizes a society whose social hierarchies and values are in serious disarray. Following the lead of Harriet Beecher Stowe, who, in *Uncle Tom's Cabin*, argued that slave traders were among the rising aristocracy of the United States, Brown has Dick Walker, a slave speculator, assume (with considerable justice) that he is on the same social and moral level as the Reverend Mr. Pinchen. This is, indeed, a realm where the slave speculator is an appropriate cultural representative, in whose office the nation's political, legal, economic, social, and religious practices meet in union. The virtues, roles, and spheres of activity associated with both male and female identity, Brown suggests, all were transformed by the system of slavery and were subject to the slave trader's authority.

REACHING THE CROSSROADS: BROWN, THE ANTISLAVERY MOVEMENT, AND THE SECOND AMERICAN REVOLUTION

This is the world into which William Wells Brown was born in 1814, on a plantation near Lexington, Kentucky. William's mother, Elizabeth, was a slave; William's father probably was related to Elizabeth's owner, Dr. John Young. The precariousness of identity for slaves was brought home to William when his owner simply changed his name to Sanford, having adopted a nephew also named William. When he escaped from slavery, "Sanford" again assumed the name of William and joined to it Wells Brown, the name of the Quaker who had aided Brown in his escape. The defining force in his life, of course, was his racial identity—a subject that Brown explores in veiled fashion in *The Escape*. In various publications and lectures, Brown retold a story that he tells in *The Escape*, of a slave child who is mistaken for the legitimate child of his slaveholder—a story Brown claimed was based on his own experience. Indeed, throughout his career as a public figure, Brown would emphasize his mixed-race status, both to emphasize the sexual and familial violations that were common under slavery and to question the stability of the color line that limited Brown's rights and activities as an American. At times, Brown could be rather inventive in his identification of his family line—for example, in his claims that he was the grandson of both Daniel Boone and Simon Lee, a Virginian slave who served in the Revolutionary War.[46] More often, Brown simply referred to his mixed-race identity as a kind of challenge to the expectations of his white audiences. In an 1855 lecture in Cincinnati, Ohio, for example, as reported in the *Anti-Slavery Bugle*, Brown began by challenging the ideological foundation of slavery, the social fiction of race, "saying that we were here to comment on the doings of our fathers. If his audience thought he referred to black fathers they were mistaken—neither did he refer to white fathers." According to the reporter of this speech, Brown then asserted that "we [are] a mixed people." But the reporter himself follows this assertion by offering a parenthetical description of Brown that emphasized the standard categories for identifying racial identity: "Mr. Brown is a light Mulatto, with a broad nose, but except [for] this and the kink in his hair, not of decidedly African features." While this description defines Brown by the degree of "African features" he both has and lacks, Brown himself insisted on defining himself, for the purposes of this speech, by the degree to which he could and could not claim his white heritage. He asserted that "his white fathers had deprived him of the privilege of appealing to the black race for his ancestry, but he was a type representing both races, and would for the moment throw aside his African ancestry, and appeal to his Anglo-Saxon." In an 1854 speech, Brown had presented essentially the same point in different terms, asserting, "I speak not now as an Anglo-Saxon, as I have a right to speak, but as an African."[47]

As he emphasized in these and similar comments in his speeches, Brown was very much a child of the slaveholding culture of nineteenth-century America, and he often talked of the education he had received by living under slavery—the lessons he had learned about human nature and about American culture. During his time as a slave, Brown witnessed the sale of his mother, sister, and brothers; and Brown was separated permanently from his mother after an unsuccessful attempt to escape with her in 1833. Brown himself was hired out to work, at various times, at a tavern, in a hotel, on a steamboat, in a printing office, as a medical assistant to Dr. Young, and as an assistant to James Walker, a slave trader. After Brown's unsuccessful attempt at escape, Young sold Brown to Enoch Price, a St. Louis merchant and steamboat owner; the following year, Brown used his new position to find another opportunity to escape in 1834. In the long and active career that followed his escape, Brown was, among other things, an antislavery lecturer and conductor of the Underground Railroad; a barber; a medical doctor of questionable expertise; an author of poems, novels, autobiographies, travel narratives, and historical studies; and a doting father of two daughters educated in Farmington, New York, and later in London.[48] Brown first went to London when he was elected as a delegate to the International Peace Congress in Paris in 1849. He stayed in London after the Fugitive Slave Law was passed in 1850, for by this time Brown was a public figure, and a return to the United States would have been dangerous.

Brown became involved in the organized antislavery movement in 1843, when he attended the National Convention of Colored Citizens of the United States in Buffalo, New York; soon thereafter, he became an agent for the Western New York Anti-Slavery Society. Brown made his first speech at the tenth anniversary meeting of the American Anti-Slavery Society in 1844, and he became a lecturing agent for the Massachusetts Anti-Slavery Society in 1847, during which year he published *Narrative of William W. Brown, A Fugitive Slave*. Published by the Boston Anti-Slavery

Office, the Narrative was a great success, with four American editions and, later, five British editions. Brown's public career was firmly established. In England, Brown lectured frequently and wrote for London newspapers. It was in England, too, that Brown published *Clotel; or, The President's Daughter: A Narrative of Slave Life in the United States*, the first novel by an African American writer. He authored two other pioneering works as well: *A Description of William Wells Brown's Original Panoramic Views of the Scenes in the Life of an American Slave, from His Birth in Slavery to His Death or His Escape to His First Home of Freedom on British Soil and Three Years in Europe; or, Places I Have Seen and People I Have Met*. Brown stayed in London until his freedom was secured by payment to his former owner, Enoch Price, in 1854; and he arrived in Boston, to a great public reception, in the fall of that year. Resuming his career as a paid antislavery lecturer, Brown began reading original dramas in 1856 and was a respected figure in the antislavery movement. Following the Civil War, Brown continued his work in the temperance movement, which he had begun in the early years following his escape; and in 1864 he began practicing medicine, following two years of reading and apprenticeship. On 6 November 1884, the author and reformer died as the result of a tumor of the bladder.

As Brown's career suggests, resistance to slavery took many forms. For those still enslaved, resistance could mean feigned incompetence, disruption of daily life, escape, or revolt. Certainly, the most notable examples of slave resistance were the planned revolts, some of which were successful enough to have a marked effect on white southern society. The best-known conspiracies (which were exposed before they could be completed) were those of Gabriel Prosser in Virginia (1800) and Denmark Vesey in South Carolina (1822); the best-known revolt was the one led by Nat Turner in Virginia (1831). Widely publicized also was the rebellion in 1839 on the Spanish slaver *Amistad*, an event that led to legal disputes, political skirmishes, and eventually a Supreme Court decision in 1841 to grant the rebels their freedom. The year 1841 saw also a slave rebellion on the slaver *Creole*, which was bound from Virginia to New Orleans. The slaves took the ship to the British colony of Nassau, where they attained their freedom. These well-known acts of conspiracy and physical resistance sent shock waves across the American political landscape, adding to the sectional tensions that increasingly defined national political life.

Following the abolition of slavery in the North, resistance in that region grew dramatically in strength and numbers in the first half of the nineteenth century. In fact, Brown escaped at a time when the organized antislavery movement was entering into a vital new phase of agitation. African

American religious and fraternal organizations long had been active in voicing resistance to slavery, and in 1830 the first national convention of blacks met in Philadelphia. This was followed by many such conventions, including the one in 1843 at which Brown listened to Henry Highland Garnet's "Address to the Slaves of the United States of America." In this talk, Garnet advised the enslaved to resist their enslavers, arguing, "There is not much hope of redemption without the shedding of blood. If you must bleed, let it all come at once—rather *die freemen than live to be slaves*."[49] White antislavery advocates also were increasingly active and organized, most notably in the establishment of William Lloyd Garrison's antislavery newspaper, *The Liberator*. Garrison was one of the most influential abolitionists; and *The Liberator*, through the publication of articles, poems, editorials, announcements, and advertisements, was a major force in shaping antislavery culture. In 1832, the New England Anti-Slavery Society was formed in Boston; in 1833, the American Anti-Slavery Society was founded in Philadelphia; in 1840, the antislavery Liberty Party was formed. When, in 1834, Great Britain abolished slavery in the West Indies, the antislavery movement in America was prepared to try to build on the momentum of that event, which African Americans commemorated annually on August 1.

The increasing presence of an organized antislavery movement is indicated by the increasingly heated responses to their calls for justice. In 1836, for example, the House of Representatives adopted a gag rule prohibiting the reception of antislavery petitions and restricting congressional debate. In 1837, the white abolitionist Elijah Lovejoy was murdered by a mob in Alton, Illinois. There were tensions within the movement as well. Resistance to some of Garrison's methods and principles led to a break in the American Anti-Slavery Society in 1840, resulting in the formation of the American and Foreign Anti-Slavery Society, an anti-Garrisonian organization. Complex, increasingly powerful, and threatened by divisions within as well as attacks from without, the antislavery movement was a diverse, sometimes unsteady, but ultimately influential force in northern life.

A paradoxically public antislavery effort was the one that made a point of its secrecy: the Underground Railroad. "The Underground Railroad," a significant presence in *The Escape*, is the term used to refer to efforts to help fugitive slaves reach relative safety in the northern states and in Canada. There are many stories about the origin of the term "Underground Railroad," but in almost all versions the term is coined by a befuddled slaveholder speculating on the successful escape of a slave. This system, as legend has it, relied on a network of "tracks" (established routes), "conductors" (people who took the slaves from one place to another), and "stations" (houses along the way, with secret passages, hiding places, and tunnels). The legend has a firm basis in fact, for regional efforts to aid fugitives often were very well organized and effective. Conductors aided fugitives along established routes; in many cities, vigilance committees watched for "slave catchers" and other dangers; many antislavery organizations provided funding (though sometimes not without considerable debate); sewing circles provided clothes to the fugitives; and secret modes of communication were established. Songs and spirituals provided a coded language; "Follow the Drinking Gourd," for example, referred to the Big Dipper and the North Star. Some slaves who escaped—most famously, Harriet Tubman and Josiah Henson—returned to the South to help others on the journey; and many white northerners also risked their lives and their freedom to go to the South to guide the fugitives.[50]

However, this legend of a single, secret organization—with officers, coded language, and Gothic passageways—sometimes has had the effect of overemphasizing the heroic efforts of white antislavery workers and obscuring the contributions of northern black individuals and communities. Moreover, stories about the Underground Railroad, told in historical studies, plays, children's books, and other publications, sometimes understate the considerable courage, ingenuity, and initiative of the escaping slaves themselves. In fact, northern black communities were important sources of communication with the South, and some escaped slaves were understandably reluctant to trust the white people they encountered in the North. Many escaping slaves made and executed their plans with no knowledge that there was any organized group of people who might help them. In other words, the legend of the Underground Railroad, when allowed to stand as a simple story about a complex past, can keep us from recognizing the considerable heroism of the slaves, many of whom found their own way northward and only then discovered and connected with an organization that could offer them shelter and protection. Indeed, in some cases, slaves who escaped entirely on their own later were listed as Underground Railroad success stories.

In the nineteenth century, however, the legend of the Underground Railroad was important in itself, for it helped to increase pressure on proslavery forces, especially in those regions closest to the North. The existence of this secret system was publicly announced in newspapers, novels, and antislavery lectures, much as Brown, in *The Escape*, celebrates its existence by devoting an episode and even a song to the Underground Railroad. The Underground Railroad was a frequent topic in the propaganda battles between proslavery and antislavery forces, and antislavery forces considered it a means of chipping away at the ideological and economic stability of the system of slavery.

Portrayals of the Underground Railroad in fiction—such as Harriet Beecher Stowe's *Uncle Tom's Cabin* or Brown's own *Clotel; or, The President's Daughter*—were based on reality, but they also were important as means of reframing the terms of the battle over slavery. The Underground Railroad helped to transform a moral and political issue into something of an adventure story, one that could play to regional pride, as the journey to the North was transformed into an allegory of the struggle for freedom. Albert Bushnell Hart, an early historian of the Underground Railroad, represented the tone of this cultural institution when he wrote in 1899 that "in aiding fugitive slaves[,] the abolitionist was making the most effective protest against the continuance of slavery; but he was also doing something more tangible; he was helping the oppressed, he was eluding the oppressor; and at the same time he was enjoying the most romantic and exciting amusement open to men who had high moral standards. He was taking risks, defying the laws, and making himself liable to punishment, and yet could glow with the healthful pleasure of duty done." Hart goes on to say, "The Underground Railroad was the opportunity for the bold and adventurous; it had the excitement of piracy, the secrecy of burglary, the daring of insurrection; to the pleasure of relieving the poor negro's sufferings it added the triumph of snapping one's fingers at the slave-catcher; it developed coolness, indifference to danger, and quickness of resource."[51] This was a story worth telling, allowing all but the slaveholders an opportunity to play a heroic role; and this story has been popular ever since—leading, in our own time, to national park projects, numerous children's books, and even a board game.

Still, other stories call for an audience, too—the accounts of those left behind in the South. Certainly, the Underground Railroad plays an important role in *The Escape*, providing Brown not only with his central plot line (the play ends with a struggle at the shore of the Niagara River) but also with a popular way to present the struggle for freedom. As we celebrate the liberation of Melinda, Glen, and Cato in *The Escape*, however, we should remember that the great majority of black characters represented directly and indirectly in this play remain enslaved, and that no Underground Railroad can carry them all to freedom. Estimates of the actual number of fugitives aided by, or credited to, the Underground Railroad range roughly from thirty to one hundred thousand. These numbers can seem significant until one remembers that millions of people remained enslaved. Frederick Douglass, certainly one who remembered, recognized the value of helping even a few fugitives escape to safety; but he recognized as well the limitations of what he always complained was an overly publicized system. Writing, years later, about his efforts to help fugitives reach Canada, Frederick Douglass noted that, "as a means of destroying slavery, it [the Underground Railroad] was like an attempt to bail out the ocean with a teaspoon."[52]

Of course, teaspoons add up after a while, and both the legend and the actuality of the Underground Railroad were part of a much larger field of activity. The increasingly vigorous legal, verbal, and physical exchanges between proslavery and antislavery forces, together with increasing political tensions between the northern and the southern states, came to a head in the 1850s, a decade during which civil war increasingly seemed inevitable.

The decade began with the so-called Compromise of 1850, an attempt to resolve sectional conflicts that served largely to heighten them. Included in this compromise measure was the Fugitive Slave Law, which allowed federal commissioners to force citizens to aid in the recapture of fugitive slaves. This law also established a process for establishing the identities of fugitives that favored slavecatchers over black northerners. The Fugitive Slave Law, both a restatement and a radical extension of the preexisting fugitive slave law, emphasized the extent to which the rights of African Americans went unrecognized in the United States Constitution and in the nation's legal processes. Some northern states quickly established personal liberty laws designed to resist the Fugitive Slave Law, but these had limited success. As a result of the Fugitive Slave Law (which made it possible for even free men and women to be "returned" to slavery), many fugitives who had settled in the northern states, as well as many African Americans who never had been enslaved, felt it necessary to leave the country.

From the middle to the end of the 1850s, the battle over slavery moved increasingly toward civil war. In 1854, Congress approved the Kansas-Nebraska Act, which allowed residents (those who were white and male) to decide whether their territory would enter the Union as a slave or free state—an act which inspired renewed violence in the territories and which in 1854 contributed to the formation of the Republican party in opposition to this extension of slavery. In 1857, the Supreme Court decision in the case of *Dred Scott v. Sanford* emphasized the extent to which the white nation was opposed to justice across racial lines. Speaking for the majority, Chief Justice Roger B. Taney stated that African Americans, whether slave or free, could not be considered citizens. The decision was vigorously opposed by the Republican party, and even Democrats disagreed over how to respond to the decision. The resulting constitutional and ideological debates ultimately helped to define the forces that led the nation into civil war.

In 1859, John Brown voiced the frustrations of many on both sides of the color line when he led a small group composed of both black and white men in an unsuccessful attempt to take control of the federal arsenal at Harper's Ferry, Virginia. Brown had hoped to provoke and support a slave insurrection by providing a protected area to which escapees could flee and from which they could extend their efforts. John Brown was hanged for treason in December 1859 and became the symbolic white martyr to the antislavery cause. Branded by many whites a zealous madman, for many blacks he seemed one of the few white heroes in America. From such early revolutionaries as Gabriel Prosser and Nat Turner to such later ones as John Brown and Harriet Tubman, many in America long had been at war over slavery. In 1861, the war spread and grew into the Civil War, or what some considered the second American Revolution. This war led to emancipation of the slaves and a new era of tenuous possibilities and thwarted justice for African Americans.

Leap to Freedom: Brown and Antislavery Culture

Given the complexity and the enormity of the slaveholding powers, and the assumption of white supremacy that shaped opinions on all sides of the debates, why would William Wells Brown decide to write and read on the antislavery lecture circuit an original dramatic work? Posing this question can remind us of the extent to which proslavery and antislavery publications shaped attitudes about slavery and race in the nineteenth century. Perhaps this question also can help us appreciate Brown's faith in the almost miraculous efficacy of words. His was not a simple faith, as Brown emphasized in an 1847 lecture to the Female Anti-Slavery Society of Salem, Massachusetts. As he put it, "Slavery has never been represented; Slavery never can be represented."[53]

Throughout his career, Brown seems to have remembered this dictum; for, more than any other nineteenth-century African American writer, Brown played with the conventions and assumptions of literary representation, never quite giving readers what they expected and almost always commenting, though in veiled fashion, on those expectations. *The Escape*, for all its apparent simplicity, is an example of the kind of writing that has earned Brown a reputation among recent scholars as a trickster narrator, someone who understands how to play upon his audience's assumptions when faced with an imbalance of power. As Jeanne R. Smith has stated, "Tricksters are masters of disguise and consummate survivors, skillfully outmaneuvering their foes with guile, wit, and charm."[54]

Foes, of course, can look like friends and can take the form of antislavery sympathizers, as well as proslavery defenders. As scholar Frances Smith
Foster has argued, "While white abolitionists were eager to privilege the
authenticity of black writers' descriptions of slavery, it was only insofar as
their descriptions confirmed what white readers had already accepted as
true."[55] African American writers, accordingly, were placed in the position
not only of presenting arguments against slavery and racism, but also of
confronting the effects of white supremacist thought, so pervasive even in
the antislavery movement. White antislavery lecturers and audiences alike
persisted in looking to fugitive slaves for stories of unimaginable cruelty,
and often they viewed the fugitives themselves largely as objects of pity,
occasions for noble sentiments. Frederick Douglass famously complains in
his 1855 autobiography, *My Bondage and My Freedom*, "I was generally
introduced as a *'chattel'*—a *'thing'*—a piece of southern *'property'*—the
chairman assuring the audience that it could speak." What Douglass experienced on the lecture circuit applied as well to responses to the published slave narratives that were so central to the antislavery cause. White
readers responded best to representations of African American identity
when these were presented as spectacles both horrifying and uplifting,
stories told either to denounce slavery or to celebrate white northern
benevolence. The task African American writers faced, then, was not only
to represent African American life and identity, but also to control the
terms of representation. Most writers would have agreed with Thomas
Hamilton, the editor of the black-oriented *Anglo-African Magazine*, who
complained in the opening editorial of that publication, "The wealth, the
intellect, the legislation (state and federal), the pulpit, and the science of
America, have concentrated on no one point so heartily as in the endeavor
to write down the negro as something less than a man."[56]

To be sure, many white writers were important in presenting the antislavery message. One of the strongest of the indictments against slavery
was *American Slavery As It Is*, a compilation of narratives, "testimonies"
by white southerners, articles from southern papers, and other forms of
evidence gathered by Theodore Weld, Angelina Grimké Weld, and
Angelina's sister, Sarah Grimké. Published in 1839, *American Slavery As
It Is* provided material for a number of subsequent antislavery writers,
William Wells Brown among them. Brown drew liberally from this book
in his own writing, often quoting verbatim in his novel *Clotel*. Other white
writers were similarly forceful in their writings—William Lloyd Garrison
in the pages of *The Liberator*; Lydia Maria Child, in *An Appeal in Favor of
That Class of Americans Called Africans* (1833), in her work as editor
of the *National Anti-Slavery Standard* (1841–43), and in various other

publications; and, of course, Harriet Beecher Stowe, in her novel, *Uncle Tom's Cabin; or, Life Among the Lowly* (1852), one of the most successful and influential publications in the nineteenth century.

The list of white writers fervently devoted to the abolition of slavery is large, but African American writers nevertheless understood that white writers were more likely to write strongly against slavery than to write knowingly against racism; and, as I have indicated, many other white writers were equally fervent in writing proslavery and white supremacist books and articles. Accordingly, it was very important to African American writers to tell their side of the story, a conviction expressed eloquently in an editorial in the first edition of the first African American newspaper, *Freedom's Journal* (1827):

> We wish to plead our own cause. Too long have others spoken for us. Too long has the public been deceived by misrepresentations, in things which concern us dearly, though in the estimation of some mere trifles; for though there are many in society who exercise towards us benevolent feelings, still (with sorrow we confess it) there are others who make it their business to enlarge upon the least trifle, which tends to the discredit of any person of color; and pronounce anathemas and denounce our whole body for the misconduct of this guilty one.

African American writers did indeed plead their own cause, often at some sacrifice. In 1829, David Walker published his uncompromising *Appeal to the Coloured Citizens of the World*, noting that, by doing so, he had put his life in danger. Southern whites protested the publication strongly and tried to prevent it from entering the South (though the book was smuggled in). When David Walker was found dead shortly after the publication of the *Appeal's* third edition in 1830, many (at that time and subsequently) suspected that Walker's death was connected with reactions to that work, although the evidence suggests that Walker died of consumption.[57] Other newspapers, pamphlets, and books followed; the number of slave narratives increased. In 1853, William Wells Brown, inspired in part by the success of *Uncle Tom's Cabin*, took African American self-representation farther still, writing a fictional narrative that has been called the first African American novel.

For both black and white writers, the purpose of antislavery writing was to promote the development of an antislavery movement, and central to such efforts were the many songs written for the cause. These songs, for the most part, were distinct from the spirituals that grew out of the slaves' experiences. Often those spirituals served the slaves as secret means of communication and, more directly, as avenues for establishing a sense of community and common culture. Most antislavery songs, in contrast, were written by antislavery advocates, who usually wrote new lyrics for established melodies, often with deliberate intent. For example, the lines

> My country, 'tis of thee,
>
> sweet land of liberty
>
> of thee I sing

were changed to

> My country, 'tis of thee,
>
> Dark land of Slavery,
>
> In thee we groan.[58]

Important collections of these songs were Jairus Lincoln's *Anti-Slavery Melodies* (1843), George W. Clark's *The Liberty Minstrel* (1844), and William Wells Brown's own *Anti-Slavery Harp* (1848, followed by an English edition in 1850).[59] Serving a purpose somewhat like that of folk songs during the Civil Rights movement of the 1950s and 1960s, these songs sometimes were sung by such groups as New Hampshire's Hutchinson Family Singers, who achieved great fame in the 1840s and the 1850s by singing about such issues as temperance, women's rights, and antislavery.

The fact that so many of these songs borrow from familiar melodies should remind us that antislavery efforts were contained within an often racist culture and that the task of representing African American identity entailed responding to the racial caricatures that were staples of American popular culture. Just as antislavery songsters rewrote patriotic ballads, so they sometimes provided new lyrics for frankly racist songs. One of the songs Brown includes in *The Escape*, for example, comes with instructions that it should be sung to the tune of "Dandy Jim."[60] The song to which he refers is "Dandy Jim from Caroline," a popular song from blackface minstrel shows.[61] The black dandy was a standard character in minstrel shows, "the proud, flashy dresser usually from the city but sometimes found on the plantation who was mocked as counterpart to his country bumpkin cousin, the plantation darkey, and who became a key stereotype throughout the rest of the century and into ours."[62] Blackface minstrelsy, known in the nineteenth century as Ethiopian minstrelsy or Negro minstrelsy, was a popular form of entertainment involving white performers who would play burlesque versions of invented black "types," the most famous of which was Jim Crow. The shows combined racist humor, music, dance, and the like in what was, by the 1840s, a rather standardized form of entertainment. Minstrel shows popularized a great number of stereotypical figures, and in the process influenced the kinds of African American characters readers would encounter in the works of such writers as Harriet Beecher Stowe, Herman Melville, Mark Twain—and William Wells Brown. There can be no doubt that Cato, one of the central characters in *The Escape* and very much the black dandy, is straight out of the blackface minstrel tradition.[63] The fact that Brown included this song, and blackface humor, in his play emphasizes the complex cultural field in which African American self-representation had to operate.

Why would Brown include a version of popular racist portrayals of black identity in his play? One answer is suggested by his reapplication of "Dandy Jim from Caroline," a song that, on the minstrel stage, is deeply and mockingly racist. In the play, it becomes an antislavery song and a commentary on the white Dr. Gaines, who in many ways can be seen as Cato's "whiteface" minstrel double. Brown uses Cato to comment also on the representative of white religion in this play, the Reverend Mr. Pinchen, both in Cato's own decision to become a preacher and in Cato's reference to Lorenzo Dow, a white Methodist preacher who (like Pinchen) reported going to heaven for observation and conversations. In short, Brown's play on minstrel stereotypes, in *The Escape* and in his other publications, is a means by which he challenges stereotypes, not only by arguing against them but also by turning them to other purposes.[64]

In a *North Star* (5 May 1848) editorial critical of northern Whigs and Democrats, Frederick Douglass noted with restrained anger, "We are fully aware that it is thought by many very improper for a 'Negro' to entertain any opinion derogatory to the conduct or character of white men; and know full well that we have our being in what is called a 'pure white Republic'—a Republic in which a white skin is considered above the criticism or scrutiny of a black man."[65] By presenting audiences with familiar figures of black caricature, Brown could undermine the assumptions upon which that caricature was grounded. Thus he was able to speak beyond what he seemed to say and so draw his audiences and readers into a discomfiting cultural house of mirrors—the house in which Brown himself had been born and raised.

Brown draws upon other traditions as well, for drama was a popular form of entertainment and increasingly one that addressed both the antislavery cause and the drive to develop forums for African American artistic expression. African American drama existed long before Brown published *The Escape*. In 1821, for example, a William A. Brown (no relation) founded the African Company, a theatrical group that performed at the African Grove Theatre in New York City, said at that time to be the third attempt "by persons of Colour" to establish a theater in New York City. William A. Brown opened the African Grove Theatre "in response to the uncongenial atmosphere of most theaters to black patrons (not to say black actors), particularly their restriction of blacks to the upper galleries." The African Company was graced by the talent of the great black actors James Hewlett and Ira Aldridge and enjoyed some success in presenting productions of Shakespeare's plays and other works, drawing both admirers and hecklers (whose activity eventually forced the closing of the African Grove). In 1823, that company presented William A. Brown's play, *The Drama of King Shotaway*, about an insurrection in the West Indies (where the playwright had been born) in the 1790s. Among black actors, Ira Aldridge's importance transcended these early efforts of black theatrical companies, for he became recognized internationally as exemplifying black genius and achievement.

Aldridge's career reveals again the extent to which black artistic expression was shaped by the demands of white supremacist culture. A white British actor, Charles Matthews, had developed a caricature said to be based on Aldridge's Shakespearean performances. Eventually, Aldridge was "besieged by whites with requests for the song Matthews had popularized" and "soon incorporated 'Opossum Up a Gum Tree' into his own performances." "We are thus confronted," as Eric Lott so aptly summarizes the situation, "with the perverse spectacle of one of Matthews' most profitable caricatures becoming one of Aldridge's most profitable performances."

White American dramatic productions, too, demonstrated an ability both to promote and to distort understandings of African Americans and of issues close to Brown's heart. By the time William Wells Brown began to write and read original plays on the antislavery lecture circuit, staged versions of Stowe's *Uncle Tom's Cabin*, for example, were greatly popular. *The Escape* shows signs of Brown's familiarity with at least one of these staged versions, George L. Aiken's 1852 adaptation of Stowe's novel. But these shows themselves were shaped by the minstrel tradition. Lott has noted "the extent to which the great mid-century vogue of 'Tom shows' owed precisely to the blackface tradition. The stage conventions of such productions, which included minstrel tunes and blackface makeup, were clearly those of minstrelsy; dramatizations of *Uncle Tom* foregrounded not only sectional conflict but also the blackface forms that had shadowed it."[66]

One can imagine William Wells Brown reflecting on race in the American theater and wondering whether it might be possible to turn the tables and give white audiences more than they bargained for. The dramatic mode enabled Brown to emphasize the cultural forces behind the conventions, and to emphasize as well the extent to which identity itself is a performance on the cultural stage. Anthropologists and sociologists long have viewed the life of individuals in society as a kind of performance. Erving Goffman, for example, in *The Presentation of Self in Everyday Life* (1959), discusses two "basic parts" of the individual: his life as a *"performer*, a harried fabricator of impressions involved in the all-too-human task of staging a performance," and his life as a *"character*, a figure, typically a fine one, whose spirit, strength, and other sterling qualities the performance was designed to evoke. The attributes of a performer and the attributes of a character are of a different order, quite basically so, yet both sets have their meaning in terms of the show that must go on."[67] Brown seems to have had a similar understanding of the performance of identity in the social world, and of the often great discrepancy between the performance one presents and the character one can claim. One of the central purposes of *The Escape*, in fact, is to emphasize that discrepancy, for the various social types who people Brown's play are rarely who they claim to be. Almost everyone in the play is involved in a deceptive performance of selfhood, acting out a culturally assigned role to veil private motivations. The most obvious performances, of course, are those of the slaves, whose behavior, when away from the surveillance of whites, reveals the extent to which they perform according to expectations. Even Cato, who seems to fulfill the nineteenth-century stereotype of a cowardly and conniving slave, often reveals that he is very much involved in a multilayered performance—especially when he seizes the opportunity to escape to Canada. And all the white characters in the play either make false claims of noble ancestry, as do Dr. and Mrs. Gaines, or otherwise misrepresent themselves to one another.

Perhaps there is yet another layer to this performance—one in which Brown's white audiences and readers were involved. Recent scholars have expanded upon the notion of social life as a kind of performance to examine the ways in which the defining concepts of identity—nationality, race, class, and gender, to note the aspects studied most frequently—themselves are shaped by complex cultural "scripts" that govern the individual's performance of selfhood. In his study of blackface minstrelsy, Lott has observed "how precariously nineteenth-century white working people"—and one can extend this to other social classes—"lived their whiteness."[68] In various ways and at various cultural levels, white Americans revealed the extent to which they were aware that their "whiteness" was inextricably linked to "blackness" and that the racial markers *white* and *black* implied boundaries that long since had been crossed. As scholar Stephen P. Knadler has argued, "Whiteness is not only a 'cultural fiction' but also a performance that is always in the process of (but never quite successful at) imitating and approximating itself." "The hegemony of white supremacy," accordingly, "depended—and still does depend—on its repetition within the 'marrow' of individual identities, on its being successfully imitated and internalized."[69] And this process of imitating and internalizing whiteness in turn depended upon concepts of blackness. Joseph Roach, a scholar of theatrical history and dramatic literature, has studied the ways in which modern cultures are deeply intertwined, joined by commerce and various forms of cultural exchange; and he has argued that modern cultures connected by Atlantic trade "invented themselves by performing their pasts in the presence of others. They could not perform themselves, however, unless they also performed what and who they thought they were not."[70] Individuals and groups, in short, define themselves in part by defining others. Moreover, these definitions entail a degree of anxiety, for, if others should resist their assigned identity, then one's own sense of self could be affected. Behind established ways of understanding the relation between the social categories *black* and *white*—categories which were inadequate to describe the complexity of American racial culture—stood a series of performances that very much involved Brown's white antislavery audiences. Confronted with Brown's representation of the cultural drama that provided their roles, the means by which they defined themselves, white northerners faced a fundamental question: what does it mean to be a white northerner?

The search for Brown's answer to this question naturally takes us to a character named Mr. White in *The Escape*, but our search should lead us to examine more broadly Brown's commentary on antislavery sentiment in this play. In *The Escape*, Brown portrays a world in which slavery provides a convenient means of distinguishing between the white North and the white South, allowing northerners to express moral sentiments without recognizing or addressing the racial prejudice pervasive among whites in both regions. By the 1850s, the antislavery media and its linked lecture circuit had become established cultural presences, and the lectures themselves were a familiar cultural ritual, with dramatic spectacles performed by fugitive slaves. Although occasionally an antislavery lecture would be an occasion for ridicule or physical attacks on the lecturer, often they were simply occasions for ideological self-affirmations on the part of white audiences accustomed to thinking that resistance to the slave system meant attending, listening, and lending financial support to antislavery lectures.[71] Aware of the need to engage such an audience, William Wells Brown sometimes would include "original panoramic views" of scenes of slavery in his lecture engagements and regularly would include antislavery songs in his performance. Henry "Box" Brown went still farther. Henry "Box" Brown had escaped from slavery by having himself shipped in a box from Richmond to Philadelphia. As a fugitive slave lecturer, Brown "included pictures of life in the South and the box in which he had made his daring escape. In England he had himself confined in the box and traveled in it from Bradford to Leeds, where he was taken out in the presence of spectators."[72] While many white audiences, no doubt, were deeply committed to the antislavery cause and were moved as much by moral outrage at the very existence of slavery as by illustrations of its violence and dehumanizing effects, still the dramatized spectacle of slavery's horrors remained a staple of antislavery culture. Joseph Roach has suggested a connection between the staging of slave auctions in New Orleans and the form of blackface minstrel shows. A subject for further examination is the connection between the minstrel shows and the staging of many antislavery events. A blend of almost religious ritual, righteous politics, sentimental spectacle, and enlightening entertainment, antislavery lectures were the high-minded talk shows of their day.

Much antislavery writing was built upon the implicit assumption that white northerners could be brought into the antislavery cause by way of an image of the North, defined in opposition to a corresponding image of the South as a land of violence and immorality. To oppose the South was to define the North as a moral and benevolent land of freedom from oppression. Antislavery sentiment itself, in other words, was a kind of self-defining performance, one very much shaped by assumptions of white supremacy. By the 1850s, especially, many African American writers condemned antislavery sympathy as a kind of benevolent neglect that veiled an underlying racial prejudice. Consider, for example, the opening statement in Rev. James Theodore Holly's *A Vindication of the Capacity of the Negro Race for Self-Government* (1857), a pamphlet defending those of African descent against charges of inferiority. Having denounced those who are openly racist, Holly complains that there exists a "large number of the noisy agitators of the present day, who would persuade themselves and the world, that they are really christian [sic] philanthropists." These "pseudo-humanitarians," Holly noted, "have lurking in their heart of hearts, a secret infidelity in regard to the real equality of the black man, which is ever ready to manifest its concealed sting, when the full and unequivocal recognition of the negro, in all respects, is pressed home upon their hearts."[73]

Both as enemies and as friends of the antislavery cause, white Americans redrew the racial lines that had been transgressed, drawing a clear distinction between Anglo-Saxon and African racial identity. As historian George Fredrickson has argued, contrasting with the "biological school" of racist thought was a school of thought promoted by those who believed themselves admirers of those of African descent. This school of thought idealized what such admirers viewed as the essential characteristics of an African race—particularly a "priority of feeling over intellect," a quality that appealed to whites who had been influenced "both by romanticism and evangelical religion." Africans and their descendants, such beliefs ran, were more emotional, more spiritual, than Anglo-Saxons. These "romantic racialists" "projected an image of the Negro that could be construed as flattering or laudatory in the context of some currently accepted ideals of human behavior and sensibility." As the antislavery movement became "fertile ground" for romantic racialists, it encouraged "benevolent reformers . . . to see the Negro more as a symbol than as a person." Since the romantic racialist school of thought assumed "essential" racial identity (qualities "in the blood"), it provided "an implicit excuse for Anglo-Saxon aggressiveness" and so "tended to undermine the notion of white moral responsibility and capability, upon which the abolitionist movement had originally placed such heavy reliance."[74]

The very sentiment that so much antislavery literature asked for, in other words, emphasized racial lines, naturalized the assumption of black dependence, and idealized white sympathy. Frustrated by the limits of this sympathy, Frederick Douglass, in 1860 in the pages of *Douglass' Monthly*, announced his support for efforts to reorganize the abolition movement, a movement that had been damaged greatly by internal divisions and philosophical differences. Noting the great need for reorganization, Douglass suggested that the movement had been stalled, in effect, by its own success in promoting antislavery sentiment in the North: "The effect of all antislavery effort thus far is this: It has filled the whole North with a sentiment opposed to slavery. Sentimental Abolitionism is abundant. It may well be met with in the pulpit, sometimes in the religious newspapers, and more frequently still we meet it in the meetings of the Republican party; yet among them all there is neither will nor purpose to abolish slavery."[75] The problem was not that antislavery sentiments were not being promoted, but rather that they *were* being both promoted and normalized among white northerners who supported the cause but resisted the implications of the message. Instead of leading white northerners to question their participation in the racial ideology central to the system of slavery, the developing culture of antislavery sentiment provided white northerners with a convenient mode of ethical self-characterization, one that avoided the issue of northern racism. In relation to the issue of slavery, what was good about a white northerner, it seemed, was that he or she was not a white southerner. As Douglass put it in 1856, "Opposing slavery and hating its victims has come to be a very common form of Abolitionism."[76]

Why write a play? Through a play, Brown could bring together all the varied aspects of American culture, as shaped by the system of slavery. *The Escape* comments on various views of race—including the use of race to justify slavery, the use of race to control the labor of the enslaved, the ways in which white southerners reveal that race is an unstable concept, and the ways in which white northerners keep the subject of race at a safe distance. *The Escape* has at its center a story of the attempted sexual violation of Melinda, as Dr. Gaines acts upon his determination to make Melinda his mistress and the vindictive Mrs. Gaines demands that Melinda commit suicide. And this story is extended by way of the many characters in the play who themselves are of mixed race, including Melinda and the slave whom a visitor takes to be the child of Dr. and Mrs. Gaines. *The Escape* enabled Brown to comment on moral decay not only in the South, but also in the North, especially through his portrait of the feeble and empty sentiments of Mr. White. Brown could comment as well on white racism, particularly in the play's reapplication of the social dynamics of blackface minstrelsy. Using this strategy, Brown turned the medium into a critique of white identity and the songs into antislavery messages. Brown also could include examples of other songs and of antislavery speeches in his play, recontextualizing them to emphasize the connection between antislavery ritual and moral principle. *The Escape* tells the story of black self-determination, as well as depicting coordinated action in the Underground Railroad. *The Escape* describes class divisions in the enslaved black, the southern white, and the northern communities, leading viewers and readers to look at these divisions for their common cultural threads. National identity, regional economics, religion, labor, race, sex, class: Brown's reach in this play is comprehensive. Seemingly simple, *The Escape* draws us into the complexity of American culture under slavery. Seemingly conventional, Brown's play leads us to question the habits of thought and assumptions that the conventions both represent and obscure.

Why a play? Perhaps, too, Brown looked for a way to change the script that he had been handed at birth. One could argue that Brown began to write and read original drama on the antislavery lecture circuit as a means of responding to a larger cultural drama in which he found himself playing a limited, pre-assigned role. In reading *The Escape*, Brown performed various roles representing identities that themselves were performances of various cultural scripts. Brown, a former slave and a northern "free black," the child of a "white" father and a "black" mother, embodied all these roles, containing within himself a collective drama of national identity. Exposing roles as roles, Brown claims the authority of the performer and not the performance, and he leaves his white audiences to contemplate the implications of their reliance on the conventions of the cultural drama of race.

Certainly it is interesting that the character in *The Escape* who is based most directly on Brown's own experiences (as suggested by his other writings) is Cato, the blackface minstrel type who is a presence throughout the play. When Cato first escapes, he is barely able to believe his good fortune. Talking to himself, he asks, "I wonder if dis is me?" This is the question Brown addresses throughout *The Escape*, turning his own performance of identity on the antislavery lecture circuit into a commentary on performance itself, including a critique of the stage upon which he stood, even as he extended that stage out to include the audience in the performance. Cato asks this question of himself and then answers *for* himself: "But maybe I is mistaken; maybe dis ain't me. Cato, is dis you? Yes, seer. Well, now it is me, an' I em a free man." Playing both roles, Cato verifies his own identity and assumes authority over his future. Brown's audience, on the other hand, is left with the same question, and with a significantly different William Wells Brown on the stage.

After securing his freedom, Cato realizes that Gaines will pursue him, so he devises a plan. "I muss change my name," he muses, "kase ole mass might foller me, and somebody might tell him dat dey seed Cato." Extending the logic of his plan, Cato determines, "So I'll change my name, and den he won't know me ef he sees me." Like Cato, Brown chose to hide in plain sight, changing his name from lecturer to playwright—making it more difficult, indeed, for his audiences to find him, and attempting to make it more difficult also for his audiences to find themselves. These many years later, *The Escape* still can help us as we continue this search.

John Ernest

NOTES

Parts of this introduction originally appeared in John Ernest, "The Reconstruction of Whiteness: William Wells Brown's *The Escape; or, A Leap for Freedom*," PMLA 113 (1998): 1108–21; and John Ernest, "Economies of Identity: Harriet E. Wilson's *Our Nig*," PMLA 109 (1994): 424–38. Reprinted by permission of the copyright owner, Modern Language Association of America.

1. William Edward Farrison, *William Wells Brown: Author and Reformer* (Chicago: Univ. of Chicago Press, 1969), 278, noting a reference in Alonzo D. Moore's "Memoir of the Author," speculates that the play originally was entitled "The Dough Face." *The Liberator* gave as the title "The Doughface Baked; or, How to Give a Northern Man a Backbone." "Don't Fail to Hear It! The Doughface Baked," *Liberator*, 23 May 1856, p. 82.

2. Nehemiah Adams, *A South-Side View of Slavery; or, Three Months at the South, in 1854* (1854; reprint, New York: Negro Universities Press, 1969), 201.

3. "Wm. Wells Brown," *Liberator*, 1 Aug. 1856, p. 124.

4. "Dramatic Readings," *National Anti-Slavery Standard*, 9 May 1857, p. 3.

5. Farrison, *William Wells Brown*, 277.

6. Henry C. Wright, "William Wells Brown—His Dramas— Their Power for Good," *Liberator*, 8 Oct. 1858, p. 163.

7. Farrison, *William Wells Brown*, 284, suggests that what was probably Brown's first public reading of *The Escape* took place in Salem, Mass., on 4 Feb. 1857. Although Brown was the first African American known to publish a play, he was not the first African American playwright. As Bernard L. Peterson Jr. has noted, "Although he was technically the third black American playwright of record, Brown was the first to be born in slavery, the first to write a full-length drama on the problems of American slavery, and the first to have a play published in the United States." Bernard L. Peterson Jr., *Early Black American Playwrights and Dramatic Writers: A Biographical Directory and Catalog of Plays, Films, and Broadcasting Scripts* (New York: Greenwood Press, 1990), 41.

8. Farrison, *William Wells Brown*, 303.

9. Ibid., 302.

10. Edmund Morgan, *American Slavery, American Freedom: The Ordeal of Colonial Virginia* (New York: Norton, 1975), 5.

11. Thomas Jefferson, *Notes on the State of Virginia* (1787; reprint, Chapel Hill: Univ. of North Carolina Press, 1982), 163.

12. The U.S. Census of 1790 listed the nation's population at 3,929,214; in 1860, the figure was 31,443,321.
13. David Christy, *Cotton Is King; or, The Culture of Cotton, and Its Relation to Agriculture, Manufactures and Commerce; and Also to the Free Colored People of the United States, and to Those Who Hold That Slavery Is in Itself Sinful*, 2d ed. (New York: Derby and Jackson, 1856), 266.
14. The word *abolitionist* itself was a word that meant different things to different people. Proslavery activists and anti-abolitionist commentators were successful in burdening this word with negative connotations and then using the word to characterize people who were not abolitionists. The northerner Christy, who opposed abolitionist efforts but was not fully in support of slavery, uses the word in this way, characterizing a wide and diverse array of northerners.
15. Perhaps the most prominent example of this vision of New England is that presented by the historian George Bancroft in his *History of the United States from the Discovery of the American Continent* (Boston: Little, Brown, 1872–74). While Bancroft was critical of some aspects of New England history, he also believed that those who colonized what would become the New England region had been motivated by faith, while those who colonized the Virginia area had been motivated by the desire for material gain. He entwined the various motivations in what proved to be a very influential theory of American history. Bancroft published the separate volumes of the history over a 40-year period, beginning in 1834, and then republished the ten-volume set in 1872–74.
16. John M. Grammer, *Pastoral and Politics in the Old South* (Baton Rouge: Louisiana State Univ. Press, 1996), 12.
17. Larry E. Tise, *Proslavery: A History of the Defense of Slavery in America, 1701–1840* (Athens: Univ. of Georgia Press, 1987), 10.
18. For useful introductions to the economics of slavery, see Richard H. Abbott, *Cotton and Capital: Boston Businessmen and Antislavery Reform, 1854–1868* (Amherst: Univ. of Massachusetts Press, 1991); Thomas Bender, ed., *The Antislavery Debate: Capitalism and Abolitionism as a Problem in Historical Interpretation* (Berkeley: Univ. of California Press, 1992); Allen Kaufman, *Capitalism, Slavery, and Republican Values: Antebellum Political Economists, 1819–1848* (Austin: Univ. of Texas Press, 1982); and Laurence Shore, *Southern Capitalists: The Ideological Leadership of an Elite, 1832–1885* (Chapel Hill: Univ. of North Carolina Press, 1986).

19. Edmund Ruffin, "The Political Economy of Slavery" in *Slavery Defended: The Views of The Old South*, ed. Eric L. McKitrick (Englewood Cliffs, N.J.: Prentice-Hall, 1963), 83.
20. George Fitzhugh, *Cannibals All! or, Slaves Without Masters* (1857; reprint, Cambridge, Mass.: Belknap Press of Harvard Univ. Press, 1960), 16.
21. See Orlando Patterson, *Slavery and Social Death: A Comparative Study* (Cambridge, Mass.: Harvard Univ. Press, 1982).
22. The pervasive influence of these elastic proslavery/anticapitalist arguments is indicated by the number of antislavery authors who felt the need to respond to such arguments. In *Uncle Tom's Cabin*, when Miss Ophelia encounters such arguments, she protests, "The English laborer is not sold, traded, parted from his family, whipped"—only to be assured by Augustine St. Clare that the two positions amount to roughly the same thing, a common condition that eventually will lead to a "mustering among the masses" and a millennial uprising. Harriet Beecher Stowe, *Uncle Tom's Cabin; or, Life among the Lowly* (1852; reprint, New York: Vintage Books/Library of America, 1991), 269–72. Understandably impatient for this eventual millennial uprising, William Wells Brown complains in *Clotel*, "Some American writers have tried to make the world believe that the condition of the labouring classes of England is as bad as the slaves of the United States." But Brown intensifies Clotel's situation to a point that allows him to emphasize that "the English labourer may be oppressed, he may be cheated, defrauded, swindled, and even starved; but it is not slavery under which he groans. He cannot be sold; in point of law he is equal to the prime minister." William Wells Brown, *Clotel; or, The President's Daughter: A Narrative of Slave Life in the United States* (1853; reprint, New York: Carol Publishing Group, 1969), 151. Similarly, Harriet A. Jacobs looks at "the poorest poor" of Europe and finds "that the condition of even the meanest and most ignorant among them was vastly superior to the condition of the most favored slaves in America." Although "their homes were very humble . . . they were protected by law." Harriet A. Jacobs, *Incidents in the Life of a Slave Girl, Written by Herself* (Cambridge, Mass.: Harvard Univ. Press, 1987), 184. Addressing a new, post–Civil War twist on the familiar problem, Mr. Thomas, in Frances E. W. Harper's *Trial and Triumph*, speaks of the "unanimity of interest" between "the white people and the colored people of this country" and warns the white merchant Mr. Hastings, "You may protect yourself from what you call the pauper of Europe,

but you will not be equally able to defend yourself from the depressed laborer of the new South, and as an American citizen, I dread any turn of the screw which will lower the rate of wages here." In Frances Smith Foster, ed., *"Minnie's Sacrifice," "Sowing and Reaping," "Trial and Triumph": Three Rediscovered Novels* by Frances E. W. Harper (Boston: Beacon Press, 1994), 222. Perhaps Harper here suggests the approach of the struggle Stowe envisioned; certainly, she points to one result of the long-sustained comparison between European laborer and the American slave—a comparison which, of course, justified little change in policy or attitude on either side of the Atlantic.

23. Adams, *South-Side View of Slavery*, 26.
24. David R. Roediger, *The Wages of Whiteness: Race and the Making of the American Working Class* (London: Verso, 1991), 66, 47, 73, 97, 100.
25. Frederick Douglass, *My Bondage and My Freedom, in Frederick Douglass: Autobiographies*, ed. Henry Louis Gates Jr. (New York: Library of America, 1994), 330.
26. Frederick Douglass, "Prejudice Against Color," in *The Life and Writings of Frederick Douglass*, vol. 2: *Pre–Civil War Decade*, ed. Philip S. Foner (New York: International Publishers, 1950), 2:128.
27. Karen Sánchez-Eppler, "Bodily Bonds: The Intersecting Rhetorics of Feminism and Abolition," in *The Culture of Sentiment: Race, Gender, and Sentimentality in Nineteenth-Century America*, ed. Shirley Samuels (New York: Oxford Univ. Press, 1992), 104. The term *miscegenation* was coined in 1863 as an anti-Republican campaign ploy.
28. John Campbell, *Negro-Mania: Being an Examination of the Falsely Assumed Equality of the Various Races of Men; Demonstrated by the Investigations of Champollion, Wilkinson, Rosellini, Van-Amringe, Gliddon, Young, Morton, Knox, Lawrence, Gen. J. H. Hammond, Murray, Smith, W. Gilmore Simms, English, Conrad, Elder, Prichard, Blumenbach, Cuvier, Brown, Le Vaillant, Carlyle, Cardinal Wiseman, Burckhardt, and Jefferson* (Philadelphia: Campbell and Power, 1851), 11–12.
29. Henry Highland Garnet, *The Past and the Present Condition, and the Destiny, of the Colored Race: A Discourse Delivered at the Fifteenth Anniversary of the Female Benevolent Society of Troy, N.Y., Feb. 14, 1848* (Troy, N.Y., 1848), 25–27.
30. Brown, *Clotel; or, The President's Daughter*, 59.
31. Jacobs, *Incidents*, 51.
32. Ibid., 53.
33. Ibid., 28.

34. Paul Gilmore, "'De Genewine Artekil': William Wells Brown, Blackface Minstrelsy, and Abolitionism," *American Literature 69*, no. 4, (1997): 759.
35. Barbara Welter, "The Cult of True Womanhood: 1820–1860," *American Quarterly* 18, no. 2 (1966): 152, identifies "four cardinal virtues" of "True Womanhood" that defined the (white) "woman's sphere" in the nineteenth century: "piety, purity, submissiveness and domesticity." Useful, though, is historian Lori D. Ginzberg's cautionary note that "the concept of 'spheres' is, after all, ideological" and "has too often come to represent historians' understanding of the actual experience of at least white middle-class Protestant women." But "the reality of women's lives was quite different from the ideology which they themselves used." Ginzberg, Women and the Work of *Benevolence: Morality, Politics, and Class in the Nineteenth-century United States* (New Haven, Conn.: Yale Univ. Press, 1990), 3.
36. Gilmore, "De Genewine Artekil," 761.
37. Hazel V. Carby, *Reconstructing Womanhood: The Emergence of the Afro-American Novelist* (New York: Oxford Univ. Press, 1987), 49.
38. Deborah Gray White, *Ar'n't I a Woman? Female Slaves in the Plantation South* (New York: W. W. Norton, 1985), 29 and 49.
39. Frederick Douglass, *Narrative of the Life of Frederick Douglass, an American Slave*, in *Frederick Douglass: Autobiographies*, ed. Henry Louis Gates Jr. (New York: Library of America, 1994), 58.
40. Joanne M. Braxton, *Black Women Writing Autobiography: A Tradition Within a Tradition* (Philadelphia: Temple Univ. Press, 1989).
41. Dorothy Sterling, *Turning the World Upside Down: The Anti-Slavery Convention of American Women* (New York: Feminist Press, 1987), 17.
42. Jacobs, *Incidents*, 50–51.
43. Jacqueline Jones, *Labor of Love, Labor of Sorrow: Black Women, Work and the Family, from Slavery to the Present* (New York: Vintage Books, 1986), 25.
44. Claudia Tate, *Domestic Allegories of Political Desire: The Black Heroine's Text at the Turn of the Century* (New York: Oxford Univ. Press, 1992), 93.
45. Brown, *Clotel*, 61.
46. See Farrison, *William Wells Brown*, 4; and William C. Nell, *The Colored Patriots of the American Revolution, with Sketches of Several Distinguished Colored Persons: To Which Is Added a Brief Survey of the Condition and Prospects of Colored Americans* (1855; reprint, Salem, N.H.: Ayer, 1986), 223.

47. "Speech by William Wells Brown, Delivered at the Cincinnati Anti-Slavery Convention, Cincinnati, Ohio, 25 April 1855," and "Speech by William Wells Brown, Delivered at the Horticultural Hall, West Chester, Pennsylvania, 23 October 1854," in *The Black Abolitionist Papers*, vol. 4: The United States, 1847–1858, ed. Peter C. Ripley (Chapel Hill: Univ. of North Carolina Press, 1991), 4:287 and 4:249.

48. The daughters, Clarissa and Josephine, were from Brown's first marriage, to Elizabeth Schooner. Married in 1834 (the same year he escaped from slavery), William and Elizabeth separated in 1847, after the couple had experienced very public marital problems. Elizabeth died in 1851, and Brown married Annie Elizabeth Gray in 1860. William and Annie had a son who died shortly after his birth in 1861, and a daughter, Clotelle, who died at the age of eight.

49. Henry Highland Garnet, "An Address to the Slaves of the United States of America," in *The Norton Anthology of African American Literature*, ed. Henry Louis Gates Jr. and Nellie Y. McKay (New York: W. W. Norton and Company, 1997), 283.

50. See, e.g., Stanley Harrold, *The Abolitionists and the South, 1831–1861* (Lexington: Univ. Press of Kentucky, 1995), which persuasively challenges the conventional wisdom that abolitionists limited their sphere of activity to the North.

51. Albert Bushnell Hart, "Introduction," in *The Underground Railroad from Slavery to Freedom*, by Wilbur H. Siebert (New York: Macmillan, 1899), viii–ix.

52. Frederick Douglass, *Life and Times of Frederick Douglass, Written by Himself*, in *Frederick Douglass: Autobiographies*, ed. Henry Louis Gates Jr. (New York: Library of America, 1994), 710.

53. William Wells Brown, *A Lecture Delivered Before the Female Anti-Slavery Society of Salem, [Massachusetts,] at Lyceum Hall, Nov. 14, 1847* (Boston: Massachusetts Anti-Slavery Society, 1847), 4.

54. Jeanne R. Smith, "Trickster," in *The Oxford Companion to African American Literature*, ed. William L. Andrews, Frances Smith Foster, and Trudier Harris (New York: Oxford Univ. Press, 1997), 736.

55. Frances Smith Foster, *Witnessing Slavery: The Development of Antebellum Slave Narratives*, 2d ed. (Madison: Univ. of Wisconsin Press, 1994), 82.

56. Thomas Hamilton, "Apology (Introductory)," *Anglo-African Magazine* [reprint, New York: Arno Press and *New York Times*, 1968] 1 (1859): 1.

57. See Peter P. Hinks, *To Awaken My Afflicted Brethren: David Walker and the Problem of Antebellum Slave Resistance* (University Park: Pennsylvania State Univ. Press, 1997), app. E: "David Walker's Death and the His-

tory of His Family." Hinks adds, "Certainly there were numerous Southerners who wanted Walker dead, and neither the possibility of murder
nor the possibility that he was stalked can be discounted" (269–70).

58. The example I am quoting here is one among many that provided
new lyrics to this song. This one comes from J. M. C. Simpson, *The
Emancipation Car, Being an Original Composition of Anti-Slavery
Ballads, Composed Exclusively for the Under Ground Rail Road*
(1874; reprint, Miami, Fla.: Mnemosyne Publishing Co., 1969), 17.

59. As Brown acknowledges in his preface to *The Anti-Slavery Harp*, he
drew many of his songs from Lincoln's *Anti-Slavery Melodies* and
Clark's *The Liberty Minstrel*.

60. Brown originally published this song, "A Song for Freedom," in *The
Anti-Slavery Harp*. In the version printed in *The Escape*, Brown omits
his original third verse, in which he identified the Constitution (rather
than the Declaration of Independence) as a document that has a clause
stating "that all men equal were created."

61. The following opening lines of "Dandy Jim from Caroline" are quoted
from Annemarie Bean, James V. Hatch, and Brooks McNamara, eds.,
*Inside the Minstrel Mask: Readings in Nineteenth-Century Blackface
Minstrelsy* (Hanover, N.H.: Wesleyan Univ. Press, 1996), 156:

> I've often heard it said ob late,
>
> Dat Souf Carolina was de state,
>
> Whara handsome nigga's bound to shine,
>
> Like Dandy Jim from Caroline.

> *Chorus:* For my ole massa tole me so,
>
> I was de best looking nigga in de country, O,
>
> I look in de glass and found 'twas so,
>
> Just what massa tole me, O.

62. Robert B. Winans, "Early Minstrel Show Music, 1843–1852," in *Inside
the Minstrel Mask: Readings in Nineteenth-Century Blackface Minstrelsy*, ed. Annemarie Bean, James V. Hatch, and Brooks McNamara
(Hanover, N.H.: Wesleyan Univ. Press, 1996), 155–56.

63. Cato resembles, e.g., the title character of John W. Smith's grotesque
and violent *The Quack Doctor* (ca. 1850). An example of blackface
minstrelsy at its lowest, *The Quack Doctor*, like *The Escape*, highlights

a "doctor" inept at pulling teeth, careless at mixing medicines, and devoted to seducing women. Black characters wearing the clothing of whites, as Cato does in *The Escape*, and mangled speech dressed up as black dialect were standard fare in white drama. These elements of ridicule went at least as far back as Robert Mumford's *The Candidates; or, The Humours of a Virginia Election* (1798), in which the black servant Ralpho is given one of his master's suits and then exclaims, "Gads! This figure of mine is not reconsiderable in its delurement."

64. Brown's use of stereotypical dialect in his portrayal of other black characters also is relevant here. The frequent puns in the dialect speeches allow Brown to comment on white culture and attitudes. Such punning was, of course, standard fare in nineteenth-century American theater, from performances of revised Shakespeare plays to blackface minstrelsy, and then to blackface minstrel versions of Shakespeare. Brown later reused material from *The Escape* in his book, *My Southern Home; Or, The South and Its People* (1880). William Andrews, discussing this material as it appears in *My Southern Home*, notes that Dolly's play on words (Susan's, in *My Southern Home*) is one of many examples "of the way in which the slaves profanely redefine the very language of authority as the whites employ it." After all, "What is the southern 'akastocacy' if not, quite literally, a *caste-ocracy*?" William Andrews, "Mark Twain, William Wells Brown, and the Problem of Authority in New South Writing," in *Southern Literature and Literary Theory*, ed. Jefferson Humphries (Athens: Univ. of Georgia Press, 1990), 12.

65. Frederick Douglass, "Northern Whigs and Democrats," in *The Life and Writings of Frederick Douglass*, vol. 1: *Early Years*, ed. Philip S. Foner (New York: International Publishers, 1950), 1:309.

66. Eric Lott, *Love and Theft: Blackface Minstrelsy and the American Working Class* (New York: Oxford Univ. Press, 1993), 44, 46, and 211.

67. Erving Goffman, *The Presentation of Self in Everyday Life* (New York: Anchor Books 1959), 252.

68. Lott, *Love and Theft*, 4.

69. Stephen P. Knadler, "Untragic Mulatto: Charles Chesnutt and the Discourse of Whiteness," *American Literary History* 8 (1996): 428–29.

70. Joseph Roach, *Cities of the Dead: Circum-Atlantic Performance* (New York: Columbia Univ. Press, 1996), 5.

71. Brown did not reject sentiment, of course, but he often included in his lectures commentary on the dangers of sentiment. In an 1855 lecture in Cincinnati, Ohio, for example, Brown told the story of how

he himself had been drawn out of his role while on a visit to "a certain town in Massachusetts." There to lecture against slavery, Brown at first was refused the use of the conservative clergyman's pulpit for the lecture. Eventually, as reported in the *Anti-Slavery Bugle*, the clergyman offered Brown the use of "both the church and the hospitality of his house." Brown hesitated to accept this grudging hospitality, in part because he planned to speak harshly against the denomination, the same as that to which his former slaveholder had belonged. But when he went to the house, "the lady of the house met him kindly, and set out the rocking chair for him," and was so kind to him that Brown decided to "cut some of the hard things I was going to say about her church." Her husband proved equally kind, and Brown decided to "scratch a little more off" his speech. More kindness was followed by additional deletions, until finally Brown "had resolved to scratch it all off, and had entirely forgotten his duty." Finally, though, seeing the couple's daughter "reminded him that he once had a sister," and then the "kindness lady of the house whose hospitality he was enjoying brought to mind his mother." In the end, "he resolved to do, and did[,] his duty." "Speech by William Wells Brown, Delivered at the Cincinnati Anti-Slavery Convention," 288–89.

72. Larry Gara, *The Liberty Line: The Legend of the Underground Railroad* (Lexington: Univ. of Kentucky Press, 1961), 121.

73. James Theodore Holly, *A Vindication of the Capacity of the Negro Race for Self-Government, and Civilized Progress, as Demonstrated by Historical Events of the Haytian Revolution; and the Subsequent Acts of That People Since Their National Independence, in Black Separatism and the Caribbean, 1860*, ed. Howard H. Bell (Ann Arbor: Univ. of Michigan Press, 1970), 21–22.

74. George M. Fredrickson, *The Black Image in the White Mind: The Debate on Afro-American Character and Destiny, 1817–1914* (New York: Harper, 1971), 101, 102, and 126.

75. Frederick Douglass, "The Abolition Movement Re-Organized," in *The Life and Writings of Frederick Douglass*, vol. 2: *Pre–Civil War Decade*, ed. Philip S. Foner (New York: International Publishers, 1950), 2:522.

76. This article is Frederick Douglass, "The Unholy Alliance of Negro Hate and Anti-Slavery," in *The Life and Writings of Frederick Douglass*, vol. 2: *Pre–Civil War Decade*, ed. Philip S. Foner (New York: International Publishers, 1950), 2:387.

A NOTE ON THE TEXT

This edition of William Wells Brown's *The Escape; or, A Leap for Freedom* follows the first edition, published in Boston in 1858 by R. F. Wallcut. The original spellings and presentations have been preserved, and I have maintained the irregularities in the spelling of words in dialect. Nor have I altered the spelling of Cato's adopted name, which drops the "g" in *Washington* the last time it appears. I have made very few and minor changes when regular patterns of presentation have been firmly established in the text. For example, character names for the dialogue are presented in italics and followed by a period, so I changed the one instance when Cato's name was followed by a dash. Major Moore uses the phrase *good-looking woman* and then refers to *fine looking-women,* and I have changed this to *fine-looking women.* But I have not altered the original text's presentation of stage directions—even in the case of the intriguing "Enter M.D." or "Exit M.D."; in other editions, this is altered to read "enter center" and "exit center."

THE

ESCAPE;

OR,

A LEAP FOR FREEDOM.

𝔄 𝔇𝔯𝔞𝔪𝔞

IN FIVE ACTS.

BY WILLIAM WELLS BROWN.

AUTHOR OF "CLOTEL," "SKETCHES OF PLACES AND PEOPLE ABROAD," ETC.

"Look on this picture, and on this." — HAMLET.

AUTHOR'S PREFACE.

This play was written for my own amusement, and not with the remotest thought that it would ever be seen by the public eye. I read it privately, however, to a circle of my friends, and through them was invited to read it before a Literary Society. Since then, the Drama has been given in various parts of the country. By the earnest solicitation of some in whose judgment I have the greatest confidence, I now present it in a printed form to the public. As I never aspired to be a dramatist, I ask no favor for it, and have little or no solicitude for its fate. If it is not readable, no word of mine can make it so: if it is, to ask favor for it would be needless.

The main features in the Drama are true. GLEN and MELINDA are actual characters, and still reside in Canada. Many of the incidents were drawn from my own experience of eighteen years at the South. The marriage ceremony, as performed in the second act, is still adhered to in many of the Southern States, especially in the farming districts.

The ignorance of the slave, as seen in the case of "BIG SALLY," is common wherever chattel slavery exists. The difficulties created in the domestic circle by the presence of beautiful slave women, as found in DR. GAINES'S family, is well understood by all who have ever visited the valley of the Mississippi.

The play, no doubt, abounds in defects, but as I was born in slavery, and never had a day's schooling in my life, I owe the public no apology for errors.

W. W. B.

CHARACTERS REPRESENTED.

DR. GAINES, *proprietor of the farm at Muddy Creek.*

REV. JOHN PINCHEN, *a clergyman.*

DICK WALKER, *a slave speculator.*

MR. WILDMARSH, *neighbor to Dr. Gaines.*

MAJOR MOORE, *a friend of Dr. Gaines.*

MR. WHITE, *a citizen of Massachusetts.*

BILL JENNINGS, *a slave speculator.*

JACOB SCRAGG, *overseer to Dr. Gaines.*

MRS. GAINES, *wife of Dr. Gaines.*

MR. and MRS. NEAL, and DAUGHTER, *Quakers, in Ohio.*

THOMAS, *Mr. Neal's hired man.*

GLEN, *slave of Mr. Hamilton, brother-in-law of Dr. Gaines.*

CATO, SAM, SAMPEY, MELINDA, DOLLY, SUSAN and BIG SALLY,
    slaves of Dr. Gaines.

PETE, NED, and BILL, *slaves.*

OFFICERS, LOUNGERS, BARKEEPER, &c.

THE ESCAPE.

ACT I.

Scene 1.—A SITTING-ROOM

MRS. GAINES, *looking at some drawings—SAMPEY, a white slave,*
stands behind the lady's chair.

Enter DR. GAINES, R.

Dr. Gaines. Well, my dear, my practice is steadily increasing. I forgot
to tell you that neighbor Wyman engaged me yesterday as his family physician; and I hope that the fever and ague, which is now taking hold of the
people, will give me more patients. I see by the New Orleans papers that
the yellow fever is raging there to a fearful extent. Men of my profession
are reaping a harvest in that section this year. I would that we could have
a touch of the yellow fever here, for I think I could invent a medicine that
would cure it. But the yellow fever is a luxury that we medical men in this
climate can't expect to enjoy; yet we may hope for the cholera.

Mrs. Gaines. Yes, I would be glad to see it more sickly here, so that
your business might prosper. But we are always unfortunate. Every body
here seems to be in good health, and I am afraid that they'll keep so.
However, we must hope for the best. We must trust in the Lord. Providence may possibly send some disease amongst us for our benefit.

Enter CATO, R.

Cato. Mr. Campbell is at de door, massa.

Dr. G. Ask him in, Cato.

Enter MR. CAMPBELL, R.

Dr. G. Good morning, Mr. Campbell. Be seated.

Mr. Campbell. Good morning, doctor. The same to you, Mrs. Gaines. Fine morning, this.

Mrs. G. Yes, sir; beautiful day.

Mr. C. Well, doctor, I've come to engage you for my family physician. I am tired of Dr. Jones. I've lost another very valuable nigger under his treatment; and, as my old mother used to say, "change of pastures makes fat calves."

Dr. G. I shall be most happy to become your doctor. Of course, you want me to attend to your niggers, as well as to your family?

Mr. C. Certainly, sir. I have twenty-three servants. What will you charge me by the year?

Dr. G. Of course, you'll do as my other patients do, send your servants to me when they are sick, if able to walk?

Mr. C. Oh, yes; I always do that.

Dr. G. Then I suppose I'll have to lump it, and say $500 per annum.

Mr. C. Well, then, we'll consider that matter settled; and as two of the boys are sick, I'll send them over. So I'll bid you good day, doctor. I would be glad if you would come over some time, and bring Mrs. Gaines with you.

Dr. G. Yes, I will; and shall be glad if you will pay us a visit, and bring with you Mrs. Campbell. Come over and spend the day.

Mr. C. I will. Good morning, doctor.

[*Exit* MR. CAMPBELL, R.

Dr. G. There, my dear, what do you think of that? Five hundred dollars more added to our income. That's patronage worth having! And I am glad to get all the negroes I can to doctor, for Cato is becoming very useful to me in the shop. He can bleed, pull teeth, and do almost any thing that the blacks require. He can put up medicine as well as any one. A valuable boy, Cato!

Mrs. G. But why did you ask Mr. Campbell to visit you, and to bring his wife? I am sure I could never consent to associate with her, for I understand that she was the daughter of a tanner. You must remember, my dear, that I was born with a silver spoon in my mouth. The blood of the Wyleys runs in my veins. I am surprised that you should ask him to visit you at all; you should have known better.

Dr. G. Oh, I did not mean for him to visit me. I only invited him for the sake of compliments, and I think he so understood it; for I should be far from wishing you to associate with Mrs. Campbell. I don't forget, my dear, the family you were raised in, nor do I overlook my own family. My father, you know, fought by the side of Washington, and I hope some day to have a handle to my own name. I am certain Providence intended me for something higher than a medical man. Ah! by-the-by, I had forgotten that I have a couple of patients to visit this morning. I must go at once.

[*Exit* DR. GAINES, R.

Enter HANNAH, L.

Mrs. G. Go, Hannah, and tell Dolly to kill a couple of fat pullets, and to put the biscuit to rise. I expect brother Pinchen here this afternoon, and I want every thing in order. Hannah, Hannah, tell Melinda to come here.

[*Exit* HANNAH, L.

We mistresses do have a hard time in this world; I don't see why the Lord should have imposed such heavy duties on us poor mortals. Well, it can't last always. I long to leave this wicked world, and go home to glory.

Enter MELINDA.

I am to have company this afternoon, Melinda. I expect brother Pinchen here, and I want every thing in order. Go and get one of my new caps, with the lace border, and get out my scolloped-bottomed dimity petti-coat, and when you go out, tell Hannah to clean the white-handled knives, and see that not a speck is on them; for I want every thing as it should be while brother Pinchen is here.

[*Exit* MRS. GAINES, L, HANNAH, R.

Scene 2.—DOCTOR'S SHOP—CATO MAKING PILLS.

Enter DR. GAINES, L.

Dr. G. Well, Cato, have you made the batch of ointment that I ordered?

Cato. Yes, massa; I dun made de intment, an' now I is making the bread pills. De tater pills is up on the top shelf.

Dr. G. I am going out to see some patients. If any gentlemen call, tell them I shall be in this afternoon. If any servants come, you attend to them. I expect two of Mr. Campbell's boys over. You see to them. Feel their pulse, look at their tongues, bleed them, and give them each a dose of calomel. Tell them to drink no cold water, and to take nothing but water gruel.

Cato. Yes, massa; I'll tend to 'em.

[*Exit* DR. GAINES, L.

Cato. I allers knowed I was a doctor, an' now de ole boss has put me at it, I muss change my coat. Ef any niggers comes in, I wants to look suspect-able. Dis jacket don't suit a doctor; I'll change it. [*Exit* CATO—*immedi-ately returning in a long coat*.] Ah! now I looks like a doctor. Now I can bleed, pull teef, or cut off a leg. Oh! well, well, ef I aint put de pill stuff an' de intment stuff togedder. By golly, dat ole cuss will be mad when he finds it out, won't he? Nebber mind, I'll make it up in pills, and when de flour is on dem, he won't know what's in 'em; an' I'll make some new intment. Ah! yonder comes Mr. Campbell's Pete an' Ned; dems de ones massa sed was comin'. I'll see ef I looks right. [*Goes to the looking-glass and views himself.*] I em some punkins, ain't I? [*Knock at the door.*] Come in.

Enter PETE *and* NED, R.

Pete. Whar is de doctor?

Cato. Here I is; don't you see me?

Pete. But whar is de ole boss?

Cato. Dat's none you business. I dun tole you dat I is de doctor, an dat's enuff.

Ned. Oh! do tell us whar de doctor is. I is almos dead. Oh me! oh dear me! I is so sick. [*Horrible faces.*]

Pete. Yes, do tell us; we don't want to stan here foolin'.

Cato. I tells you again dat I is de doctor. I larn de trade under massa.

Ned. Oh! well, den, give me somethin' to stop dis pain. Oh dear me! I shall die. [*He tries to vomit, but can't— ugly faces.*]

Cato. Let me feel your pulse. Now put out your tongue. You is berry sick. Ef you don't mine, you'll die. Come out in de shed, an' I'll bleed you. [*Exit all—re-enter.*

Cato. Dar, now take dese pills, two in de mornin' and two at night, and ef you don't feel better, double de dose. Now, Mr. Pete, what's de matter wid you?

Pete. I is got de cole chills, an' has a fever in de night.

Cato. Come out, an' I'll bleed you.

[*Exit all—re-enter.*

Now take dese pills, two in de mornin' and two at night, an' ef dey don't help you, double de dose. Ah! I like to forget to feel your pulse and look at your tongue. Put out your tongue. [*Feels his pulse.*] Yes, I tells by de feel ob your pulse dat I is gib you de right pills.

Enter MR. Parker's BILL, L.

Cato. What you come in dat door widout knockin' for?

Bill. My toof ache so, I didn't tink to knock. Oh, my toof! my toof! Whar is de doctor?

Cato. Here I is; don't you see me?

Bill. What! you de doctor, you brack cuss! You looks like a doctor! Oh, my toof! my toof! Whar is de doctor?

Cato. I tells you I is de doctor. Ef you don't believe me, ax dese men. I can pull your toof in a minnit.

Bill. Well, den, pull it out. Oh, my toof! how it aches! Oh, my toof! [*Cato gets the rusty turnkeys.*]

Cato. Now lay down on your back.

Bill. What for?

Cato. Dat's de way massa does.

Bill. Oh, my toof! Well, den, come on. [*Lies down, Cato gets astraddle of Bill's breast, puts the turnkeys on the wrong tooth, and pulls—Bill kicks, and cries out*]— Oh, do stop! Oh! oh! oh! [*Cato pulls the wrong tooth—Bill jumps up.*

Cato. Dar, now, I tole you I could pull your toof for you.

Bill. Oh, dear me! Oh, it aches yet! Oh me! Oh, Lor-e-massy! You dun pull de wrong toof. Drat your skin! ef I don't pay you for this, you brack cuss! [*They fight, and turn over table, chairs and bench—Pete and Ned look on.*

Enter DR. GAINES, R.

Dr. G. Why, dear me, what's the matter? What's all this about? I'll teach you a lesson, that I will. [*The doctor goes at them with his cane.*

Cato. Oh, massa! he's to blame, sir. He's to blame. He struck me fuss.

Bill. No, sir; he's to blame; he pull de wrong toof. Oh, my toof! oh, my toof!

Dr. G. Let me see your tooth. Open your mouth. As I live, you've taken out the wrong tooth. I am amazed. I'll whip you for this; I'll whip you well. You're a pretty doctor. Now lie down, Bill, and let him take out the right tooth; and if he makes a mistake this time, I'll cowhide him well. Lie down, Bill. [*Bill lies down, and Cato pulls the tooth.*] There now, why didn't you do that in the first place?

Cato. He wouldn't hole still, sir.

Bill. He lies, sir. I did hole still.

Dr. G. Now go home, boys; go home.

[*Exit* PETE, NED *and* BILL, L.

Dr. G. You've made a pretty muss of it, in my absence. Look at the table! Never mind, Cato; I'll whip you well for this conduct of yours today. Go to work now, and clear up the office.

[*Exit* DR. GAINES, R.

Cato. Confound dat nigger! I wish he was in Ginny. He bite my finger and scratch my face. But didn't I give it to him? Well, den, I reckon I did. [*He goes to the mirror, and discovers that his coat is torn—weeps.*] Oh, dear me! Oh, my coat—my coat is tore! Dat nigger has tore my coat. [*He gets angry, and rushes about the room frantic.*] Cuss dat nigger! Ef I

could lay my hands on him, I'd tare him all to pieces,—dat I would. An'
de ole boss hit me wid his cane after dat nigger tore my coat. By golly, I
wants to fight somebody. Ef ole massa should come in now, I'd fight him.
[*Rolls up his sleeves.*] Let 'em come now, ef dey dare—ole massa, or any
body else; I'm ready for 'em.

Enter DR. GAINES, R.

Dr. G. What's all this noise here?

Cato. Nuffin', sir; only jess I is puttin' things to rights, as you tole me.
I didn't hear any noise except de rats.

Dr. G. Make haste, and come in; I want you to go to town.

[*Exit* DR. GAINES, R.

Cato. By golly, de ole boss like to cotch me dat time, didn't he? But was
n't I mad? When I is mad, nobody can do nuffin' wid me. But here's my
coat, tore to pieces. Cuss dat nigger! [*Weeps.*] Oh, my coat! oh, my coat! I
rudder he had broke my head den to tore my coat. Drat dat nigger! Ef he
ever comes here agin, I'll pull out every toof he's got in his head—dat I will.

[*Exit,* R.

Scene 3.—A ROOM IN THE QUARTERS.

Enter GLEN, L.

Glen. How slowly the time passes away. I've been waiting here two
hours, and Melinda has not yet come. What keeps her, I cannot tell. I
waited long and late for her last night, and when she approached, I sprang
to my feet, caught her in my arms, pressed her to my heart, and kissed
away the tears from her moistened cheeks. She placed her trembling hand
in mine, and said, "Glen, I am yours; I will never be the wife of another."
I clasped her to my bosom, and called God to witness that I would ever
regard her as my wife. Old Uncle Joseph joined us in holy wedlock by
moonlight; that was the only marriage ceremony. I look upon the vow as
ever binding on me, for I am sure that a just God will sanction our union
in heaven. Still, this man, who claims Melinda as his property, is unwilling
for me to marry the woman of my choice, because he wants her himself.
But he shall not have her. What he will say when he finds that we are
married, I cannot tell; but I am determined to protect my wife or die. Ah!
here comes Melinda.

Enter MELINDA, R.

I am glad to see you, Melinda. I've been waiting long, and feared you
would not come. Ah! in tears again?

Melinda. Glen, you are always thinking I am in tears. But what did
master say to-day?

Glen. He again forbade our union.

Melinda. Indeed! Can he be so cruel?

Glen. Yes, he can be just so cruel.

Melinda. Alas! alas! how unfeeling and heartless! But did you appeal to his generosity?

Glen. Yes, I did; I used all the persuasive powers that I was master of, but to no purpose; he was inflexible. He even offered me a new suit of clothes, if I would give you up; and when I told him that I could not, he said he would flog me to death if I ever spoke to you again.

Melinda. And what did you say to him?

Glen. I answered, that, while I loved life better than death, even life itself could not tempt me to consent to a separation that would make life an unchanging curse. Oh, I would kill myself, Melinda, if I thought that, for the sake of life, I could consent to your degradation. No, Melinda, I can die, but shall never live to see you the mistress of another man. But, my dear girl, I have a secret to tell you, and no one must know it but you. I will go out and see that no person is within hearing. I will be back soon.

[*Exit* GLEN, L.

Melinda. It is often said that the darkest hour of the night precedes the dawn. It is ever thus with the vicissitudes of human suffering. After the soul has reached the lowest depths of despair, and can no deeper plunge amid its rolling, fœtid shades, then the reactionary forces of man's nature begin to operate, resolution takes the place of despondency, energy succeeds instead of apathy, and an upward tendency is felt and exhibited. Men then hope against power, and smile in defiance of despair. I shall never forget when first I saw Glen. It is now more than a year since he came here with his master, Mr. Hamilton. It was a glorious moonlight night in autumn. The wide and fruitful face of nature was silent and buried in repose. The tall trees on the borders of Muddy Creek waved their leafy branches in the breeze, which was wafted from afar, refreshing over hill and vale, over the rippling water, and the waving corn and wheat fields. The starry sky was studded over with a few light, flitting clouds, while the moon, as if rejoicing to witness the meeting of two hearts that should be cemented by the purest love, sailed triumphantly along among the shifting vapors.

Oh, how happy I have been in my acquaintance with Glen! That he loves me, I do well believe it; that I love him, it is most true. Oh, how I would that those who think the slave incapable of the finer feelings, could only see our hearts, and learn our thoughts,—thoughts that we dare not utter in the presence of our masters! But I fear that Glen will be separated from me, for there is nothing too base and mean for master to do, for the purpose of getting me entirely in his power. But, thanks to Heaven, he does not own Glen, and therefore cannot sell him. Yet he might purchase him from his brother-in-law, so as to send him out of the way. But here comes my husband.

Enter GLEN, L.

Glen. I've been as far as the overseer's house, and all is quiet. Now, Melinda, as you are my wife, I will confide to you a secret. I've long been thinking of making my escape to Canada, and taking you with me. It is true that I don't belong to your master, but he might buy me from Hamilton, and then sell me out of the neighborhood.

Melinda. But we could never succeed in the attempt to escape.

Glen. We will make the trial, and show that we at least deserve success. There is a slave trader expected here next week, and Dr. Gaines would sell you at once if he knew that we were married. We must get ready and start, and if we can pass the Ohio river, we'll be safe on the road to Canada.

[*Exit,* R.

Scene 4.—DINING-ROOM.

REV. MR. PINCHEN *giving* MRS. GAINES *an account of his experience as a minister*—HANNAH *clearing away the breakfast table*—SAMPEY *standing behind* Mrs. GAINES' *chair.*

Mrs. Gaines. Now, do give me more of your experience, brother Pinchen. It always does my soul good to hear religious experience. It draws me nearer and nearer to the Lord's side. I do love to hear good news from God's people.

Mr. Pinchen. Well, sister Gaines, I've had great opportunities in my time to study the heart of man. I've attended a great many camp-meetings, revival meetings, protracted meetings, and death-bed scenes, and I am satisfied, sister Gaines, that the heart of man is full of sin, and desperately wicked. This is a wicked world, sister Gaines, a wicked world.

Mrs. G. Were you ever in Arkansas, brother Pinchen? I've been told that the people out there are very ungodly.

Mr. P. Oh, yes, sister Gaines. I once spent a year at Little Rock, and preached in all the towns round about there; and I found some hard cases out there, I can tell you. I was once spending a week in a district where there were a great many horse thieves, and one night, somebody stole my pony. Well, I knowed it was no use to make a fuss, so I told brother Tarbox to say nothing about it, and I'd get my horse by preaching God's everlasting gospel; for I had faith in the truth, and knowed that my Savior would not let me lose my pony. So the next Sunday I preached on horse-stealing, and told the brethren to come up in the evenin' with their hearts filled with the grace of God. So that night the house was crammed brim full with anxious souls, panting for the bread of life. Brother Bingham opened with prayer, and brother Tarbox followed, and I saw right off that we were gwine to have a blessed time. After I got 'em pretty well warmed up, I jumped on to one of the seats, stretched out my hands, and said, "I know who stole my pony; I've found out; and you are in here tryin' to make people believe that you've got religion; but you ain't got it. And if you don't take my horse back to brother Tarbox's pasture this very night, I'll tell your name right out in meetin' to-morrow night. Take my pony back, you vile and wretched sinner, and come up here and give your heart to God." So the next mornin', I went out to brother Tarbox's pasture, and sure enough, there was my bobtail pony. Yes, sister Gaines, there he was, safe and sound. Ha, ha, ha.

Mrs. G. Oh, how interesting, and how fortunate for you to get your pony! And what power there is in the gospel! God's children are very lucky. Oh, it is so sweet to sit here and listen to such good news from God's people! You Hannah, what are you standing there listening for, and neglecting your work? Never mind, my lady, I'll whip you well when I am done here. Go at your work this moment, you lazy huzzy! Never mind, I'll whip you well. [*Aside.*] Come, do go on, brother Pinchen, with your godly conversation. It is so sweet! It draws me nearer and nearer to the Lord's side.

Mr. P. Well, sister Gaines, I've had some mighty queer dreams in my time, that I have. You see, one night I dreamed that I was dead and in heaven, and such a place I never saw before. As soon as I entered the gates of the celestial empire, I saw many old and familiar faces that I had seen before. The first person that I saw was good old Elder Pike, the preacher that first called my attention to religion. The next person I saw was Deacon Billings, my first wife's father, and then I saw a host of godly faces. Why, sister Gaines, you knowed Elder Goosbee, didn't you?

Mrs. G. Why, yes; did you see him there? He married me to my first husband.

Mr. P. Oh, yes, sister Gaines, I saw the old Elder, and he looked for all the world as if he had just come out of a revival meetin'.

Mrs. G. Did you see my first husband there, brother Pinchen?

Mr. P. No, sister Gaines, I didn't see brother Pepper there; but I've no doubt but that brother Pepper was there.

Mrs. G. Well, I don't know; I have my doubts. He was not the happiest man in the world. He was always borrowing trouble about something or another. Still, I saw some happy moments with Mr. Pepper. I was happy when I made his acquaintance, happy during our courtship, happy a while after our marriage, and happy when he died. [*Weeps.*]

Hannah. Massa Pinchen, did you see my ole man Ben up dar in hebben?

Mr. P. No, Hannah; I didn't go amongst the niggers.

Mrs. G. No, of course brother Pinchen didn't go among the blacks. What are you asking questions for? Never mind, my lady, I'll whip you well when I'm done here. I'll skin you from head to foot. [*Aside.*] Do go on with your heavenly conversation, brother Pinchen; it does my very soul good. This is indeed a precious moment for me. I do love to hear of Christ and Him crucified.

Mr. P. Well, sister Gaines, I promised sister Daniels that I'd come over and see her this morning, and have a little season of prayer with her, and I suppose I must go. I'll tell you more of my religious experience when I return.

Mrs. G. If you must go, then I'll have to let you; but before you do, I wish to get your advice upon a little matter that concerns Hannah. Last week, Hannah stole a goose, killed it, cooked it, and she and her man Sam had a fine time eating the goose; and her master and I would never have known a word about it, if it had not been for Cato, a faithful servant, who told his master. And then, you see, Hannah had to be severely whipped before she'd confess that she stole the goose. Next Sabbath is sacrament day, and I want to know if you think that Hannah is fit to go to the Lord's supper after stealing the goose.

Mr. P. Well, sister Gaines, that depends on circumstances. If Hannah has confessed that she stole the goose, and has been sufficiently whipped, and has begged her master's pardon, and begged your pardon, and thinks she'll never do the like again, why then I suppose she can go to the Lord's supper; for

"While the lamp holds out to burn,
The vilest sinner may return."

But she must be sure that she has repented, and won't steal any more.

Mrs. G. Now, Hannah, do you hear that? For my own part, I don't think she's fit to go to the Lord's supper, for she had no occasion to steal the goose. We give our niggers plenty of good wholesome food. They have a full run to the meal tub, meat once a fortnight, and all the sour milk about the place, and I'm sure that's enough for any one. I do think that our niggers are the most ungrateful creatures in the world, that I do. They aggravate my life out of me.

Hannah. I know, missis, dat I steal de goose, and massa whip me for it, and I confess it, and I is sorry for it. But, missis, I is gwine to de Lord's supper, next Sunday, kase I ain't agwine to turn my back on my bressed Lord an' Massa for no old tough goose, dat I ain't. [*Weeps.*]

Mr. P. Well, sister Gaines, I suppose I must go over and see sister Daniels; she'll be waiting for me.

[*Exit* Mr. PINCHEN, M.D.

Mrs. G. Now, Hannah, brother Pinchen is gone, do you get the cowhide and follow me to the cellar, and I'll whip you well for aggravating me as you have to-day. It seems as if I can never sit down to take a little comfort with the Lord, without you crossing me. The devil always puts it into your head to disturb me, just when I am trying to serve the Lord. I've no doubt but that I'll miss going to heaven on your account. But I'll whip you well before I leave this world, that I will. Get the cowhide and follow me to the cellar.

[*Exit* MRS. GAINES *and* HANNAH, R.

--------·-·•--------

ACT II.

Scene 1.—PARLOR.

DR. GAINES *at a table, letters and papers before him.*

Enter SAMPEY, L.

Sampey. Dar's a gemman at de doe, massa, dat wants to see you, seer.

Dr. Gaines. Ask him to walk in, Sampey.

[*Exit* SAMPEY, L.

Enter WALKER.

Walker. Why, how do you do, Dr. Gaines? I em glad to see you, I'll swear.

Dr. G. How do you do, Mr. Walker? I did not expect to see you up here so soon. What has hurried you?

Walk. Well, you see, doctor, I comes when I em not expected. The price of niggers is up, and I em gwine to take advantage of the times. Now, doctor, ef you've got any niggers that you wants to sell, I em your man. I am paying the highest price of any body in the market. I pay cash down, and no grumblin'.

Dr. G. I don't know that I want to sell any of my people now. Still, I've got to make up a little money next month, to pay in bank; and another thing, the doctors say that we are likely to have a touch of the cholera this summer, and if that's the case, I suppose I had better turn as many of my slaves into cash as I can.

Walk. Yes, doctor, that is very true. The cholera is death on slaves, and a thousand dollars in your pocket is a great deal better than a nigger in the field, with cholera at his heels. Why, who is that coming up the lane? It's Mr. Wildmarsh, as I live! Jest the very man I wants to see.

Enter MR. WILDMARSH.

Why, how do you do, Squire? I was jest a thinkin' about you.

Wildmarsh. How are you, Mr. Walker? and how are you, doctor? I am glad to see you both looking so well. You seem in remarkably good health, doctor?

Dr. G. Yes, Squire, I was never in the enjoyment of better health. I hope you left all well at Licking?

Wild. Yes, I thank you. And now, Mr. Walker, how goes times with you?

Walk. Well, you see, Squire, I em in good spirits. The price of niggers is up in the market, and I am lookin' out for bargains; and I was jest intendin' to come over to Lickin' to see you, to see if you had any niggers to sell. But it seems as ef the Lord knowed that I wanted to see you, and directed your steps over here. Now, Squire, ef you've got any niggers you wants to sell, I em your man. I am payin' the highest cash price of any body in the market. Now's your time, Squire.

Wild. No, I don't think I want to sell any of my slaves now. I sold a very valuable gal to Mr. Haskins last week. I tell you, she was a smart one. I got eighteen hundred dollars for her.

Walk. Why, Squire, how you do talk! Eighteen hundred dollars for one gal? She must have been a screamer to bring that price. What sort of a lookin' critter was she? I should like to have bought her.

Wild. She was a little of the smartest gal I've ever raised; that she was.

Walk. Then she was your own raising, was she?

Wild. Oh, yes; she was raised on my place, and if I could have kept her three or four years longer, and taken her to the market myself, I am sure I could have sold her for three thousand dollars. But you see, Mr. Walker, my wife got a little jealous, and you know jealousy sets the women's heads a teetering, and so I had to sell the gal. She's got straight hair, blue eyes, prominent features, and is almost white. Haskins will make a spec, and no mistake.

Walk. Why, Squire, was she that pretty little gal that I saw on your knee the day that your wife was gone, when I was at your place three years ago?

Wild. Yes, the same.

Walk. Well, now, Squire, I thought that was your daughter; she looked mightily like you. She was your daughter, wasn't she? You need not be ashamed to own it to me, for I am mum upon such matters.

Wild. You know, Mr. Walker, that people will talk, and when they talk, they say a great deal; and people did talk, and many said the gal was my daughter; and you know we can't help people's talking. But here comes the Rev. Mr. Pinchen; I didn't know that he was in the neighborhood.

Walk. It is Mr. Pinchen, as I live; jest the very man I wants to see.

Enter MR. PINCHEN, R.

Why, how do you do, Mr. Pinchen? What in the name of Jehu brings you down here to Muddy Creek? Any camp-meetins, revival meetins, death-bed scenes, or any thing else in your line going on down here? How is religion prosperin' now, Mr. Pinchen? I always like to hear about religion.

Mr. Pin. Well, Mr. Walker, the Lord's work is in good condition every where now. I tell you, Mr. Walker, I've been in the gospel ministry these thirteen years, and I am satisfied that the heart of man is full of sin and desperately wicked. This is a wicked world, Mr. Walker, a wicked world, and we ought all of us to have religion. Religion is a good thing to live by, and we all want it when we die. Yes, sir, when the great trumpet blows, we ought to be ready. And a man in your business of buying and selling slaves needs religion more than any body else, for it makes you treat your people as you should. Now, there is Mr. Haskins,—he is a slave-trader, like your-self. Well, I converted him. Before he got religion, he was one of the worst men to his niggers I ever saw; his heart was as hard as stone. But religion has made his heart as soft as a piece of cotton. Before I converted him, he would sell husbands from their wives, and seem to take delight in it; but now he won't sell a man from his wife, if he can get any one to buy both of them together. I tell you, sir, religion has done a wonderful work for him.

Walk. I know, Mr. Pinchen, that I ought to have religion, and I feel that I am a great sinner; and whenever I get with good pious people like you and the doctor, and Mr. Wildmarsh, it always makes me feel that I am a desperate sinner. I feel it the more, because I've got a religious turn of mind. I know that I would be happier with religion, and the first spare time I get, I am going to try to get it. I'll go to a protracted meeting, and I won't stop till I get religion. Yes, I'll scuffle with the Lord till I gets forgiven. But it always makes me feel bad to talk about religion, so I'll change the subject. Now, doctor, what about them thar niggers you thought you could sell me?

Dr. Gaines. I'll see my wife, Mr. Walker, and if she is willing to part with Hannah, I'll sell you Sam and his wife, Hannah. Ah! here comes my wife; I'll mention it.

Enter MRS. GAINES, L.

Ah! my dear, I am glad you've come. I was just telling Mr. Walker, that if you were willing to part with Hannah, I'd sell him Sam and Hannah.

Mrs. G. Now, Dr. Gaines, I am astonished and surprised that you should think of such a thing. You know what trouble I've had in training up Hannah for a house servant, and now that I've got her so that she knows my ways, you want to sell her. Hav n't you niggers enough on the plantation to sell, without selling the servants from under my very nose?

Dr. G. Oh, yes, my dear; but I can spare Sam, and don't like to separate him from his wife; and I thought if you could let Hannah go, I'd sell them both. I don't like to separate husbands from their wives.

Mrs. G. Now, gentlemen, that's just the way with my husband. He thinks more about the welfare and comfort of his slaves, than he does of himself or his family. I am sure you need not feel so bad at the thought of separating Sam from Hannah. They've only been married eight months, and their attachment can't be very strong in that short time. Indeed, I shall be glad if you do sell Sam, for then I'll make Hannah *jump the broomstick* with Cato, and I'll have them both here under my eye. I never will again let one of my house servants marry a field hand—never! For when night comes on, the servants are off to the quarters, and I have to holler and holler enough to split my throat before I can make them hear. And another thing: I want you to sell Melinda. I don't intend to keep that mulatto wench about the house any longer.

Dr. Gaines. My dear, I'll sell any servant from the place to suit you, except Melinda. I can't think of selling her—I can't think of it.

Mrs. G. I tell you that Melinda shall leave this house, or I'll go. There, now you have it. I've had my life tormented out of me by the presence of that yellow wench, and I'll stand it no longer. I know you love her more than you do me, and I'll—I'll—I'll write—write to my father. [*Weeps.*]

[*Exit* MRS. GAINES, L.

Walk. Why, doctor, your wife's a screamer, ain't she? Ha, ha, ha. Why, doctor, she's got a tongue of her own, ain't she? Why, doctor, it was only last week that I thought of getting a wife myself; but your wife has skeered the idea out of my head. Now, doctor, if you wants to sell the gal, I'll buy her. Husband and wife ought to be on good terms, and your wife won't feel well till the gal is gone. Now, I'll pay you all she's worth, if you wants to sell.

Dr. G. No, Mr. Walker; the girl my wife spoke of is not for sale. My wife does not mean what she says; she's only a little jealous. I'll get brother Pinchen to talk to her, and get her mind turned upon religious matters, and then she'll forget it. She's only a little jealous.

Walk. I tell you what, doctor, ef you call that a little jealous, I'd like to know what's a heap. I tell you, it will take something more than religion to set your wife right. You had better sell me the gal; I'll pay you cash down, and no grumblin'.

Dr. G. The girl is not for sale, Mr. Walker; but if you want two good, able-bodied servants, I'll sell you Sam and Big Sally. Sam is trustworthy, and Sally is worth her weight in gold for rough usage.

Walk. Well, doctor, I'll go out and take a look at 'em, for I never buys slaves without examining them well, because they are sometimes injured by over-work or under-feedin'. I don't say that is the case with yours, for I don't believe it is; but as I sell on honor, I must buy on honor.

Dr. G. Walk out, sir, and you can examine them to your heart's content. Walk right out, sir.

Scene 2.—VIEW IN FRONT OF THE GREAT HOUSE.

Examination of SAM *and* BIG SALLY.—DR. GAINES, WILDMARSH,

MR. PINCHEN *and* WALKER *present.*

Walk. Well, my boy, what's your name?

Sam. Sam, sir, is my name.

Walk. How old are you, Sam?

Sam. Ef I live to see next corn plantin' time, I'll be 27, or 30, or 35, or 40—I don't know which, sir.

Walk. Ha, ha, ha. Well, doctor, this is rather a green boy. Well, mer feller, are you sound?

Sam. Yes, sir, I spec I is.

Walk. Open your mouth and let me see your teeth. I allers judge a nigger's age by his teeth, same as I dose a hoss. Ah! pretty good set of grinders. Have you got a good appetite?

Sam. Yes, sir.

Walk. Can you eat your allowance?

Sam. Yes, sir, when I can get it.

Walk. Get out on the floor and dance; I want to see if you are supple.

Sam. I don't like to dance; I is got religion.

Walk. Oh, ho! you've got religion, have you? That's so much the better. I likes to deal in the gospel. I think he'll suit me. Now, mer gal, what's your name?

Sally. I is Big Sally, sir.

Walk. How old are you, Sally?

Sally. I don't know, sir; but I heard once dat I was born at sweet pertater diggin' time.

Walk. Ha, ha, ha. Don't know how old you are! Do you know who made you?

Sally. I hev heard who it was in de Bible dat made me, but I dun forget de gentman's name.

Walk. Ha, ha, ha. Well, doctor, this is the greenest lot of niggers I've seen for some time. Well, what do you ask for them?

Dr. Gaines. You may have Sam for $1000, and Sally for $900. They are worth all I ask for them. You know I never banter, Mr. Walker. There they are; you can take them at that price, or let them alone, just as you please.

Walk. Well, doctor, I reckon I'll take 'em; but it's all they are worth. I'll put the handcuffs on 'em, and then I'll pay you. I likes to go accordin' to Scripter. Scripter says ef eatin' meat will offend your brother, you must quit it; and I say, ef leavin' your slaves without the handcuffs will make 'em run away, you must put the handcuffs on 'em. Now, Sam, don't you and Sally cry. I am of a tender heart, and it allers makes me feel bad to see people cryin'. Don't cry, and the first place I get to, I'll buy each of you a great big *ginger cake,*—that I will. Now, Mr. Pinchen, I wish you were going down the river. I'd like to have your company; for I allers likes the company of preachers.

Mr. Pinchen. Well, Mr. Walker, I would be much pleased to go down the river with you, but it's too early for me. I expect to go to Natchez in four or five weeks, to attend a camp-meetin', and if you were going down then, I'd like it. What kind of niggers sells best in the Orleans market, Mr. Walker?

Walk. Why, field hands. Did you think of goin' in the trade?

Mr. P. Oh, no; only it's a long ways down to Natchez, and I thought I'd just buy five or six niggers, and take 'em down and sell 'em to pay my travellin' expenses. I only want to clear my way.

Scene 3.—SITTING-ROOM—TABLE AND ROCKING-CHAIR.

Enter MRS. GAINES, R, *followed by* SAMPEY.

Mrs. Gaines. I do wish your master would come; I want supper. Run to the gate, Sampey, and see if he is coming.

[*Exit* SAMPEY, L.

That man is enough to break my heart. The patience of an angel could not stand it.

Enter SAMPEY, L.

Samp. Yes, missis, master is coming.

Enter DR. GAINES, L.

[*The Doctor walks about with his hands under his coat, seeming very much elated.*]

Mrs. Gaines. Why, doctor, what is the matter?

Dr. Gaines. My dear, don't call me *doctor.*

Mrs. G. What should I call you?

Dr. G. Call me Colonel, my dear—Colonel. I have been elected Colonel of the Militia, and I want you to call me by my right name. I always felt that Providence had designed me for something great, and He has just begun to shower His blessings upon me.

Mrs. G. Dear me, I could never get to calling you Colonel; I've called you Doctor for the last twenty years.

Dr. G. Now, Sarah, if you will call me Colonel, other people will, and I want you to set the example. Come, my darling, call me Colonel, and I'll give you any thing you wish for.

Mrs. G. Well, as I want a new gold watch and bracelets, I'll commence now. Come, Colonel, we'll go to supper. Ah! now for my new shawl. [*Aside.*] Mrs. Lemme was here to-day, Colonel, and she had on, Colonel, one of the prettiest shawls, Colonel, I think, Colonel, that I ever saw, Colonel, in my life, Colonel. And there is only one, Colonel, in Mr. Watson's store, Colonel; and that, Colonel, will do, Colonel, for a Colonel's wife.

Dr. G. Ah! my dear, you never looked so much the lady since I've known you. Go, my darling, get the watch, bracelets and shawl, and tell them to charge them to Colonel Gaines; and when you say "Colonel," always emphasize the word.

Mrs. G. Come, Colonel, let's go to supper.

Dr. G. My dear, you're a jewel,—you are!　　　　[*Exit,* R.

Enter CATO, L.

Cato. Why, whar is massa and missis? I tought dey was here. Ah! by golly, yonder comes a mulatter gal. Yes, it's Mrs. Jones's Tapioca. I'll set up to dat gal, dat I will.

Enter TAPIOCA, R.

Good ebenin', Miss Tappy. How is your folks?

Tapioca. Pretty well, I tank you.

Cato. Miss Tappy, dis wanderin' heart of mine is yours. Come, take a seat! Please to squze my manners; love discommodes me. Take a seat. Now, Miss Tappy, I loves you; an ef you will jess marry me, I'll make you a happy husband, dat I will. Come, take me as I is.

Tap. But what will Big Jim say?

Cato. Big Jim! Why, let dat nigger go to Ginny. I want to know, now, if you is tinkin' about dat common nigger? Why, Miss Tappy, I is surstonished dat you should tink 'bout frowin' yousef away wid a common, ugly lookin' cuss like Big Jim, when you can get a fine lookin', suspectable man like me. Come, Miss Tappy, choose dis day who you have. Afore I go any furder, give me one kiss. Come, give me one kiss. Come, let me kiss you.

Tap. No you shan't—dare now! You shan't kiss me widout you is stronger den I is and I know you is dat. [*He kisses her.*]

Enter DR. GAINES, R, *and hides.*

Cato. Did you know, Miss Tappy, dat I is de head doctor 'bout dis house? I beats de ole boss all to pieces.

Tap. I hev hearn dat you bleeds and pulls teef.

Cato. Yes, Miss Tappy; massa could not get along widout me, for massa was made a doctor by books; but I is a natral doctor. I was born a doctor, jess as Lorenzo Dow was born a preacher. So you see I can't be nuffin' but a doctor, while massa is a bunglin' ole cuss at de bissness.

Dr. Gaines, (in a low voice.) Never mind; I'll teach you a lesson, that I will.

Cato. You see, Miss Tappy, I was gwine to say—Ah! but afore I forget, jess give me anudder kiss, jess to keep company wid de one dat you give me jess now,—dat's all. [*Kisses her.*] Now, Miss Tappy, duse you know de fuss time dat I seed you?

Tap. No, Mr. Cato, I don't.

Cato. Well, it was at de camp-meetin'. Oh, Miss Tappy, dat pretty red calliker dress you had on dat time did de work for me. It made my heart flutter—

Dr. G. (low voice.) Yes, and I'll make your black hide flutter.

Cato. Didn't I hear some noise? By golly, dar is teves in dis house, and I'll drive 'em out. [*Takes a chair and runs at the Doctor, and knocks him down. The Doctor chases Cato round the table.*

Cato. Oh, massa, I didn't know 'twas you!

Dr. G. You scoundrel! I'll whip you well. Stop! I tell you.

[*Curtain falls.*

ACT III.

Scene 1.—SITTING-ROOM.

MRS. GAINES, *seated in an arm chair, reading a letter.*

Enter HANNAH, L.

Mrs. Gaines. You need not tell me, Hannah, that you don't want another husband, I know better. Your master has sold Sam, and he's gone down the river, and you'll never see him again. So, go and put on your calico dress, and meet me in the kitchen. I intend for you to *jump the broomstick* with Cato. You need not tell me that you don't want another man. I know that there's no woman living that can be happy and satisfied without a husband.

Hannah. Oh, missis, I don't want to jump de broomstick wid Cato. I don't love Cato; I can't love him.

Mrs. G. Shut up, this moment! What do you know about love? I didn't love your master when I married him, and people don't marry for love now. So go and put on your calico dress, and meet me in the kitchen.

[*Exit* HANNAH, L.

I am glad that the Colonel has sold Sam; now I'll make Hannah marry Cato, and I have them both here under my eye. And I am also glad that the Colonel has parted with Melinda. Still, I'm afraid that he is trying to deceive me. He took the hussy away yesterday, and says he sold her to a trader; but I don't believe it. At any rate, if she's in the neighborhood, I'll find her, that I will. No man ever fools me.

[*Exit* MRS. GAINES, L.

Scene 2.—THE KITCHEN—SLAVES AT WORK.

Enter HANNAH, R.

Hannah. Oh, Cato, do go and tell missis dat you don't want to jump de broomstick wid me,—dat's a good man! Do, Cato; kase I nebber can love you. It was only las week dat massa sold my Sammy, and I don't want any udder man. Do go tell missis dat you don't want me.

Cato. No, Hannah, I ain't a gwine to tell missis no such thing, kase I dose want you, and I ain't a-gwine to tell a lie for you ner nobody else. Dar, now you's got it! I don't see why you need to make so much fuss. I is better lookin' den Sam; an' I is a house servant, an' Sam was only a fiel hand; so you ought to feel proud of a change. So go and do as missis tells you.

[*Exit* HANNAH, L.

Hannah needn't try to get me to tell a lie; I ain't a-gwine to do it, kase I dose want her, an' I is bin wantin' her dis long time, an' soon as massa sold Sam, I knowed I would get her. By golly, I is gwine to be a married man. Won't I be happy! Now, ef I could only jess run away from ole massa, an' get to Canada wid Hannah, den I'd show 'em who I was. Ah! dat reminds me of my song 'bout ole massa and Canada, an' I'll sing it fer yer. Dis is my moriginal hyme. It comed into my head one night when I was fass asleep under an apple tree, looking up at de moon. Now for my song:—

AIR—*"Dandy Jim."*

Come all ye bondmen far and near,

Let's put a song in massa's ear,

It is a song for our poor race,

Who're whipped and trampled with disgrace.

CHORUS.

My old massa tells me, Oh,

This is a land of freedom, Oh;

Let's look about and see if it's so,

Just as massa tells me, Oh.

He tells us of that glorious one,

I think his name was Washington,

How he did fight for liberty,

To save a threepence tax on tea. [*Chorus.*]

But now we look about and see

That we poor blacks are not so free;

We're whipped and thrashed about like fools,

And have no chance at common schools. [*Chorus.*]

They take our wives, insult and mock,

And sell our children on the block,

They choke us if we say a word,

And say that "niggers" shan't be heard. [*Chorus.*]

Our preachers, too, with whip and cord,

Command obedience in the Lord;

They say they learn it from the big book,

But for ourselves, we dare not look. [*Chorus.*]

There is a country far away,

I think they call it Canada,

And if we reach Victoria's shore,

They say that we are slaves no more.

Now haste, all bondmen, let us go,

And leave this *Christian* country, Oh;

Haste to the land of the British Queen,

Where whips for negroes are not seen.

Now, if we go, we must take the night,

And never let them come in sight;

The bloodhounds will be on our track,

And wo to us if they fetch us back.

Now haste all bondmen, let us go,

And leave this *Christian* country, Oh;

God help us to Victoria's shore,

Where we are free and slaves no more!

Enter MRS. GAINES, L.

Mrs. Gaines. Ah! Cato, you're ready, are you? Where is Hannah?

Cato. Yes, missis; I is bin waitin' dis long time. Hannah has bin here tryin' to swade me to tell you dat I don't want her; but I telled her dat you sed I must jump de broomstick wid her, an' I is gwine to mind you.

Mrs. G. That's right, Cato; servants should always mind their masters and mistresses, without asking a question.

Cato. Yes, missis, I allers dose what you and massa tells me, an' axes nobody.

Enter HANNAH, R.

Mrs. Gaines. Ah! Hannah; come, we are waiting for you. Nothing can be done till you come.

Hannah. Oh, missis, I do n't want to jump de broomstick wid Cato; I can't love him.

Mrs. G. Shut up, this moment. Dolly, get the broom. Susan, you take hold of the other end. There, now hold it a little lower—there, a little higher. There, now, that'll do. Now Hannah, take hold of Cato's hand. Let Cato take hold of your hand.

Hannah. Oh, missis, do spare me. I do n't want to jump de broomstick wid Cato.

Mrs. G. Get the cowhide, and follow me to the cellar, and I'll whip you well. I'll let you know how to disobey my orders. Get the cowhide, and follow me to the cellar.

[*Exit* MRS. GAINES *and* HANNAH, R.

Dolly. Oh, Cato, do go an' tell missis dat you don't want Hannah. Don't you hear how she's whippin' her in de cellar? Do go an' tell missis dat you don't want Hannah, and den she'll stop whippin' her.

Cato. No, Dolly, I ain't a-gwine to do no such a thing, kase ef I tell missis dat I don't want Hannah, den missis will whip me; an' I ain't a-gwine to be whipped fer you, ner Hannah, ner nobody else. No, I'll jump de broomstick wid every woman on de place, ef missis wants me to, before I'll be whipped.

Dolly. Cato, ef I was in Hannah's place, I'd see you in de bottomless pit before I'd live wid you, you great big wall-eyed, empty-headed, knock-kneed fool. You're as mean as your devilish old missis.

Cato. Ef you do n't quit dat busin' me, Dolly, I'll tell missis as soon as she comes in, an' she'll whip you, you know she will.

Enter MRS. GAINES *and* HANNAH, R.

[Mrs. G. fans herself with her handkerchief, and appears fatigued.]

Mrs. G. You ought to be ashamed of yourself, Hannah, to make me fatigue myself in this way, to make you do your duty. It's very naughty in you, Hannah. Now, Dolly, you and Susan get the broom, and get out in the middle of the room. There, hold it a little lower—a little higher; there, that'll do. Now, remember that this is a solemn occasion; you are going to jump into matrimony. Now, Cato, take hold of Hannah's hand. There, now, why could n't you let Cato take hold of your hand before? Now get ready, and when I count three, do you jump. Eyes on the *broomstick!* All ready. One, two, three, and over you go. There, now you're husband and wife, and if you do n't live happy together, it's your own fault; for I am sure there's nothing to hinder it. Now, Hannah, come up to the house, and I'll give you some whiskey, and you can make some apple toddy, and you and Cato can have a fine time.

[Exit MRS. GAINES *and* HANNAH, L.

Dolly. I tell you what, Susan, when I get married, I is gwine to have a preacher to marry me. I ain't a-gwine to jump de broomstick. Dat will do for fiel' hands, but house servants ought to be 'bove dat.

Susan. Well, chile, you can't speck any ting else from ole missis. She come from down in Carlina, from 'mong de poor white trash. She don't know any better. You can't speck nothin' more dan a jump from a frog. Missis says she is one of de akastocacy; but she ain't no more of an akastocacy dan I is. Missis says she was born wid a silver spoon in her mouf; ef she was, I wish it had a-choked her, dat's what I wish. Missis wanted to make Linda jump de broomstick wid Glen, but massa ain't a-gwine to let Linda jump de broomstick wid anybody. He's gwine to keep Linda fer heself.

Dolly. You know massa took Linda 'way las' night, an' tell missis dat he has sold her and sent her down de river; but I do n't b'lieve he has sold her at all. He went ober towards de poplar farm, an' I tink Linda is ober dar now. Ef she is dar, missis'll find it out, fer she tell'd massa las' night, dat ef Linda was in de neighborhood, she'd find her.

              [*Exit* DOLLY *and* SUSAN.

Scene 3—SITTING ROOM—CHAIRS AND TABLE.

Enter HANNAH, R.

Hannah. I don't keer what missis says; I don't like Cato, an' I won't live wid him. I always love my Sammy, an' I loves him now. [*Knock at the door—goes to the door.*

Enter MAJ. MOORE, M.D.

Walk in, sir; take a seat. I'll call missis, sir; massa is gone away.

              [*Exit* HANNAH, R.

Maj. Moore. So I am here at last, and the Colonel is not at home. I hope his wife is a good-looking woman. I rather like fine-looking women, especially when their husbands are from home. Well, I've studied human nature to some purpose. If you wish to get the good will of a man, do n't praise his wife, and if you wish to gain the favor of a woman, praise her children, and swear that they are the picture of their father, whether they are or not. Ah! here comes the lady.

Enter MRS. GAINES, R.

Mrs. G. Good morning, sir!

Maj. M. Good morning, madam! I am Maj. Moore, of Jefferson. The Colonel and I had seats near each other in the last Legislature.

Mrs. G. Be seated, sir. I think I've heard the Colonel speak of you. He's away, now; but I expect him every moment. You're a stranger here, I presume?

Maj. M. Yes, madam, I am. I rather like the Colonel's situation here.

Mrs. G. It is thought to be a fine location.

Enter SAMPEY, R.

Hand me my fan, will you, Sampey? *[Sampey gets the fan and passes near the Major, who mistakes the boy for the Colonel's son. He reaches out his hand.*

Maj. M. How do you do, bub? Madam, I should have known that this was the Colonel's son, if I had met him in California; for he looks so much like his papa.

Mrs. G. [*To the boy.*] Get out of here this minute. Go to the kitchen.

              [*Exit* SAMPEY, R.

That is one of the niggers, sir.

Maj. M. I beg your pardon, madam; I beg your pardon.

Mrs. G. No offence, sir; mistakes will be made. Ah! here comes the Colonel.

Enter DR. GAINES, M.D.

Dr. Gaines. Bless my soul, how are you, Major? I'm exceedingly pleased to see you. Be seated, be seated, Major.

Mrs. G. Please excuse me, gentlemen; I must go and look after dinner, for I've no doubt that the Major will have an appetite for dinner, by the time it is ready.

[Exit MRS. GAINES, R.

Maj. M. Colonel, I'm afraid I've played the devil here to-day.

Dr. G. Why, what have you done?

Maj. M. You see, Colonel, I always make it a point, wherever I go, to praise the children, if there are any, and so to-day, seeing one of your little servants come in, and taking him to be your son, I spoke to your wife of the marked resemblance between you and the boy. I am afraid I've insulted madam.

Dr. G. Oh! do n't let that trouble you. Ha, ha, ha. If you did call him my son, you did n't miss it much. Ha, ha, ha. Come, we'll take a walk, and talk over matters about old times.

[Exit, L.

Scene 4.—FOREST SCENERY.

Enter GLEN, L.

Glen. Oh, how I want to see Melinda! My heart pants and my soul is moved whenever I hear her voice. Human tongue cannot tell how my heart yearns toward her. Oh, God! thou who gavest me life, and implanted in my bosom the love of liberty, and gave me a heart to love, Oh, pity the poor outraged slave! Thou, who canst rend the veil of centuries, speak, Oh, speak, and put a stop to this persecution! What is death, compared to slavery? Oh, heavy curse, to have thoughts, reason, taste, judgment, conscience and passions like another man, and not have equal liberty to use them! Why was I born with a wish to be free, and still be a slave? Why should I call another man master? And my poor Melinda, she is taken away from me, and I dare not ask the tyrant where she is. It is childish to stand here weeping. Why should my eyes be filled with tears, when my brain is on fire? I will find my wife—I will; and wo to him who shall try to keep me from her!

Scene 5.—ROOM IN A SMALL COTTAGE ON THE POPLAR FARM,

(Ten miles from Muddy Creek, and owned by Dr. Gaines.)

Enter MELINDA, R.

Melinda. Here I am, watched, and kept a prisoner in this place. Oh, I would that I could escape, and once more get with Glen. Poor Glen! He does not know where I am. Master took the opportunity, when Glen was in the city with his master, to bring me here to this lonely place, and fearing that mistress would know where I was, he brought me here at night. Oh, how I wish I could rush into the arms of sleep!—that sweet sleep, which visits all alike, descending, like the dews of heaven upon the bond as well as the free. It would drive from my troubled brain the agonies of this terrible night.

Enter DR. GAINES, L.

Dr. Gaines. Good evening, Melinda! Are you not glad to see me?

Melinda. Sir, how can I be glad to see one who has made life a burden, and turned my sweetest moments into bitterness?

Dr. G. Come, Melinda, no more reproaches! You know that I love you, and I have told you, and I tell you again, that if you will give up all idea of having Glen for a husband, I will set you free, let you live in this cottage, and be your own mistress, and I'll dress you like a lady. Come, now, be reasonable!

Melinda. Sir, I am your slave; you can do as you please with the avails of my labor, but you shall never tempt me to swerve from the path of virtue.

Dr. G. Now, Melinda, that black scoundrel Glen has been putting these notions into your head. I'll let you know that you are my property, and I'll do as I please with you. I'll teach you that there is no limit to my power.

Melinda. Sir, let me warn you that if you compass my ruin, a woman's bitterest curse will be laid upon your head, with all the crushing, withering weight that my soul can impart to it; a curse that shall cling to you throughout the remainder of your wretched life; a curse that shall haunt you like a spectre in your dreams by night, and attend upon you by day; a curse, too, that shall embody itself in the ghastly form of the woman whose chastity you will have outraged. Command me to bury myself in yonder stream, and I will obey you. Bid me do any thing else, but I beseech you not to commit a double crime,—outrage a woman, and make her false to her husband.

Dr. G. You got a husband! Who is your husband, and when were you married?

Melinda. Glen is my husband, and I've been married four weeks. Old Uncle Joseph married us one night by moonlight. I see you are angry; I pray you not to injure my husband.

Dr. G. Melinda, you shall never see Glen again. I have bought him from Hamilton, and I will return to Muddy Creek, and roast him at the stake. A black villain, to get into my way in that manner! Here I've come ten miles tonight to see you, and this is the way you receive me!

Melinda. Oh, master, I beg you not to injure my husband! Kill me, but spare him! Do! do! he is my husband!

Dr. G. You shall never see that black imp again, so good night, my lady! When I come again, you'll give me a more cordial reception. Good night!

[*Exit* DR. GAINES, L.

Melinda. I shall go distracted. I cannot remain here and know that Glen is being tortured on my account. I must escape from this place,—I must,—I must!

Enter CATO, R.

Cato. No, you ain't a-gwine to 'scape, nudder. Massa tells me to keep dese eyes on you, an' I is gwine to do it.

Melinda. Oh, Cato, do let me get away! I beg you, do!

Cato. No; I tells you massa telled me to keep you safe; an' ef I let you go, massa will whip me.

[*Exit* CATO, L.

Enter MRS. GAINES, R.

Mrs. G. Ah, you trollop! here you are! Your master told me that he had sold you and sent you down the river, but I knew better; I knew it was a lie. And when he left home this evening, he said he was going to the city on business, and I knew that was a lie too, and determined to follow him, and see what he was up to. I rode all the way over here to-night. My side-saddle was lent out, and I had to ride ten miles bare-back, and I can scarcely walk; and your master has just left here. Now deny that, if you dare.

Melinda. Madam, I will deny nothing which is true. Your husband has just gone from here, but God knows that I am innocent of any thing wrong with him.

Mrs. G. It's a lie! I know better. If you are innocent, what are you doing here, cooped up in this cottage by yourself? Tell me that!

Melinda. God knows that I was brought here against my will, and I beg that you will take me away.

Mrs. G. Yes, Melinda, I will see that you are taken away, but it shall be after a fashion that you won't like. I know that your master loves you, and I intend to put a stop to it. Here, drink the contents of this vial,—drink it!

Melinda. Oh, you will not take my life,—you will not!

Mrs. G. Drink the poison this moment!

Melinda. I cannot drink it.

Mrs. G. I tell you to drink this poison at once. Drink it, or I will thrust this knife to your heart! The poison or the dagger, this instant! [*She draws a dagger; Melinda retreats, to the back of the room, and seizes a broom.*

Melinda. I will not drink the poison! [*They fight;* MELINDA *sweeps off* MRS. GAINES,—*cap, combs and curls.*

Curtain falls.

ACT IV.

Scene 1.—INTERIOR OF A DUNGEON—GLEN IN CHAINS

Glen. When I think of my unmerited sufferings, it almost drives me mad. I struck the doctor, and for that, I must remain here loaded with chains. But why did he strike me? He takes my wife from me, sends her off, and then comes and beats me over the head with his cane. I did right to strike him back again. I would I had killed him. Oh! there is a volcano pent up in the hearts of the slaves of these Southern States that will burst forth ere long. When that day comes, wo to those whom its unpitying fury may devour! I would be willing to die, if I could smite down with these chains every man who attempts to enslave his fellow-man.

Enter SAMPEY, R.

Sampey. Glen, I jess bin hear massa call de oberseer, and I spec somebody is gwine to be whipped. Anudder ting: I know whar massa took Linda to. He took her to de poplar farm, an' he went away las' night, an' missis she follow after massa, an' she ain't come back yet. I tell you, Glen, de debil will be to pay on dis place, but don't you tell any body dat I tole you.

[*Exit* SAMPEY, R.

Scene 2.—PARLOR.

DR. GAINES, *alone.*

Dr. Gaines. Yes, I will have the black rascal well whipped, and then I'll sell him. It was most fortunate for me that Hamilton was willing to sell him to me.

Enter MR. SCRAGG, L.

I have sent for you, Mr. Scragg. I want you to take Glen out of the dungeon, take him into the tobacco house, fasten him down upon the stretcher, and give him five hundred lashes upon his bare back; and when you have whipped him, feel his pulse, and report to me how it stands, and if he can bear more, I'll have you give him an additional hundred or two, as the case may be.

Scragg. I tell you, doctor, that suits me to a charm. I've long wanted to whip that nigger. When your brother-in-law came here to board, and brought that boy with him, I felt bad to see a nigger dressed up in such fine clothes, and I wanted to whip him right off. I tell you, doctor, I had rather whip that nigger than go to heaven, any day,—that I had!

Dr. G. Go, Mr. Scragg, and do your duty. Don't spare the whip!

Scragg. I will, sir; I'll do it in order.

[*Exit* SCRAGG, L.

Dr. G. Every thing works well now, and when I get Glen out of the way, I'll pay Melinda another visit, and she'll give me a different reception. But I wonder where my wife is? She left word that she was going to see her brother, but I am afraid that she has got on my track. That woman is the pest of my life. If there's any place in heaven for her, I'd be glad if the Lord would take her home, for I've had her too long already. But what noise is that? What can that be? What is the matter?

Enter SCRAGG, L., *with face bloody.*

Scragg. Oh, dear me! oh, my head! That nigger broke away from me, and struck me over the head with a stick. Oh, dear me! Oh!

Dr. G. Where is he, Mr. Scragg?

Scragg. Oh! sir, he jumped out of the window; he's gone. Oh! my head; he's cracked my skull. Oh, dear me, I'm kilt! Oh! oh! oh!

Enter SLAVES, R.

Dr. G. Go, Dolly, and wash Mr. Scragg's head with some whiskey, and bind it up. Go at once. And Bob, you run over to Mr. Hall, and tell him to come with his hounds; we must go after the rascal.

[*Exit all except the* DOCTOR, R.

This will never do. When I catch the scoundrel, I'll make an example of him; I'll whip him to death. Ah! here comes my wife. I wonder what she comes now for? I must put on a sober face, for she looks angry.

Enter MRS. GAINES, L.

Ah! my dear, I am glad you've come, I've been so lonesome without you. Oh! Sarah, I do n't know what I should do if the Lord should take you home to heaven. I do n't think that I should be able to live without you.

Mrs. G. Dr. Gaines, you ought to be ashamed to sit there and talk in that way. You know very well that if the Lord should call me home to glory to-night, you'd jump for joy. But you need not think that I am going to leave this world before you. No; with the help of the Lord, I'll stay here to foil you in your meanness. I've been on your track, and a dirty track it is, too. You ought to be ashamed of yourself. See what promises you made me before we were married; and this is the way you keep your word. When I married you, every body said that it was a pity that a woman of my sweet temper should be linked to such a man as you. [*She weeps and wrings her hands.*

Dr. G. Come, my dear, do n't make a fool of yourself. Come, let's go to supper, and a strong cup of tea will help your head.

Mrs. G. Tea help my head! tea won't help my head. You're a brute of a man; I always knew I was a fool for marrying you. There was Mr Comstock, he wanted me, and he loved me, and he said I was an angel, so he did; and he loved me, and he was rich; and mother always said that he loved me more than you, for when he used to kiss me, he always squeezed my hand. You never did such a thing in your life. [*She weeps and wrings her hands.*

Dr. G. Come, my dear, do n't act so foolish.

Mrs. G. Yes; every thing I do is foolish. You're a brute of a man; I won't live with you any longer. I'll leave you—that I will. I'll go and see a lawyer, and get a divorce from you—so I will.

Dr. G. Well, Sarah, if you want a divorce, you had better engage Mr. Barker. He's the best lawyer in town; and if you want some money to facilitate the business, I'll draw a check for you.

Mrs. G. So you want me to get a divorce, do you? Well, I won't have a divorce; no, I'll never leave you, as long as the Lord spares me.

[*Exit* MRS. GAINES, R.

Scene 3.—FOREST AT NIGHT—LARGE TREE.

Enter MELINDA, L.

Melinda. This is indeed a dark night to be out and alone on this road. But I must find my husband, I must. Poor Glen! if he only knew that I was here, and could get to me, he would. What a curse slavery is! It separates husbands from their wives, and tears mothers from their helpless off-spring, and blights all our hopes for this world. I must try to reach Muddy Creek before daylight, and seek out my husband. What's that I hear? — footsteps? I'll get behind this tree.

Enter GLEN, R.

Glen. It is so dark, I'm afraid I've missed the road. Still, this must be the right way to the poplar farm. And if Bob told me the truth, when he said that Melinda was at the poplar farm, I will soon be with her; and if I once get her in my arms, it will be a strong man that shall take her from me. Aye, a dozen strong men shall not be able to wrest her from my arms. [*Melinda rushes from behind the tree.*

Melinda. Oh, Glen! It is my husband,—it is!

Glen. Melinda! Melinda! it is, it is. Oh God! I thank Thee for this manifestation of Thy kindness. Come, come, Melinda, we must go at once to Canada. I escaped from the overseer, whom Dr. Gaines sent to flog me. Yes, I struck him over the head with his own club, and I made the wine flow freely; yes, I pounded his old skillet well for him, and then jumped out of the window. It was a leap for freedom. Yes, Melinda, it was a leap for freedom. I've said "master" for the last time. I am free; I'm bound for Canada. Come, let's be off, at once, for the negro dogs will be put upon our track. Let us once get beyond the Ohio river, and all will be right.

[*Exit* R.

ACT V.

Scene 1.—BAR-ROOM IN THE AMERICAN HOTEL—TRAVELERS LOUNGING IN CHAIRS, AND AT THE BAR.

Enter BILL JENNINGS, R.

Barkeeper. Why, Jennings, how do you do?

Jennings. Say Mr. Jennings, if you please.

Barkeeper. Well, Mr. Jennings, if that suits you better. How are times? We've been expecting you, for some days.

Jennings. Well, before I talk about the times, I want my horses put up, and want you to tell me where my niggers are to stay to-night. Sheds, stables, barns, and every thing else here, seems pretty full, if I am a judge.

Barkeeper. Oh! I'll see to your plunder.

1st Lounger. I say, Barkeeper, make me a brandy cocktail, strong. Why, how do you do, Mr. Jennings?

Jennings. Pretty well, Mr. Peters. Cold evening, this.

1st Loun. Yes, this is cold. I heard you speak of your niggers. Have you got a pretty large gang?

Jennings. No, only thirty-three. But they are the best that the country can afford. I shall clear a few dimes, this trip. I hear that the price is up.

Enter MR. WHITE, R.

White. Can I be accommodated here to-night, landlord?

Barkeeper. Yes, sir; we've bed for man and beast. Go, Dick, and take the gentleman's coat and hat. [*To the waiter.*] You're a stranger in these parts, I rec'on.

White. Yes, I am a stranger here.

2d Loun. Where mout you come from, ef it's a far question?

White. I am from Massachusetts.

3d Loun. I say, cuss Massachusetts!

1st Loun. I say so too. There is where the fanatics live; cussed traitors. The President ought to hang 'em all.

White. I say, landlord, if this is the language that I am to hear, I would like to go into a private room.

Barkeeper. We ain't got no private room empty.

1st. Loun. Maybe you're mad 'bout what I said 'bout your State. Ef you is, I've only to say that this is a free country, and people talks what they please; an' ef you do n't like it, you can better yourself.

White. Sir, if this is a free country, why do you have slaves here? I saw a gang at the door, as I came in.

2d Loun. He did n't mean that this was a free country for niggers. He meant that it's free for white people. And another thing, ef you get to talking 'bout freedom for niggers, you'll catch what you won't like, mister. It's right for niggers to be slaves.

White. But I saw some white slaves.

1st Loun. Well, they're white niggers.

White. Well, sir, I am from a free State, and I thank God for it; for the worst act that a man can commit upon his fellow-man, is to make him a slave. Conceive of a mind, a living soul, with the germs of faculties which infinity cannot exhaust, as it first beams upon you in its glad morning of existence, quivering with life and joy, exulting in the glorious sense of its developing energies, beautiful, and brave, and generous, and joyous, and free,—the clear pure spirit bathed in the auroral light of its unconscious immortality,—and then follow it in its dark and dreary passage through slavery, until oppression stifles and kills, one by one, every inspiration and aspiration of its being, until it becomes a dead soul entombed in a living frame!

3d Loun. Stop that; stop that, I say. That's treason to the country; that's downright rebellion.

Barkeeper. Yes, it is. And another thing,—this is not a meeting-house.

1st Loun. Yes, if you talk such stuff as that, you'll get a chunk of cold lead in you, that you will.

Enter DR. GAINES *and* SCRAGG, followed *by* CATO, R.

Dr. G. Gentlemen, I am in pursuit of two valuable slaves, and I will pay five hundred dollars for their arrest.

[*Exit* MR. WHITE, L.

1st Loun. I'll bet a picayune that your niggers have been stolen by that cussed feller from Massachusetts. Don't you see he's gone?

Dr. G. Where is the man? If I can lay my hands on him, he'll never steal another nigger. Where is the scoundrel?

1st Loun. Let's go after the feller. I'll go with you. Come, foller me.

[*Exit all*, L., *except* CATO *and the waiter.*

Cato. Why don't you bring in massa's saddle-bags? What de debil you standin' dar for? You common country niggers don't know nuffin', no how. Go an' get massa's saddle-bags, and bring 'em in.

[*Exit* SERVANT, R.

By golly! ebry body's gone, an' de bar-keeper too. I'll tend de bar myself now; an' de fuss gemman I waits on will be dis gemman of color. [*Goes behind the counter, and drinks.*] Ah, dis is de stuff fer me; it makes my head swim; it makes me happy right off. I'll take a little more.

Enter BARKEEPER, L.

Barkeeper. What are you doing behind that bar, you black cuss?

Cato. I is lookin' for massa's saddle-bags, sir. Is dey here?

Barkeeper. But what were you drinking there?

Cato. Me drinkin'! Why, massa, you muss be mistaken. I ain't drink nuffin'.

Barkeeper. You infernal whelp, to stand there and lie in that way!

Cato. Oh, yes, seer, I did tase dat coffee in dat bottle; dat's all I did.

Enter MR. WHITE, L., *excited.*

Mr. White. I say, sir, is there no place of concealment in your house? They are after me, and my life is in danger. Say, sir, can't you hide me away?

Barkeeper. Well, you ought to hold your tongue when you come into our State.

Mr. White. But, sir, the Constitution gives me the right to speak my sentiments, at all times and in all places.

Barkeeper. We don't care for Constitutions nor nothin' else. We made the Constitution, and we'll break it. But you had better hide away; they are coming, and they'll lynch you, that they will. Come with me; I'll hide you in the cellar. Foller me.

[*Exit* BARKEEPER *and* WHITE, L.

Enter the MOB, R.

Dr. Gaines. If I can once lay my hands on that scoundrel, I'll blow a hole through his head.

Jennings. Yes, I say so too; for no one knows whose niggers are safe, now-a-days. I must look after my niggers. Who is that I see in the distance? I believe it's that cussed Massachusetts feller. Come, let's go after him.

[*Exit the* MOB, R.

Scene 2.—FOREST AT NIGHT.

Enter GLEN *and* MELINDA, R.

Melinda. I am so tired and hungry, that I cannot go further. It is so cloudy that we cannot see the North Star, and therefore cannot tell whether we are going to Canada, or further South. Let's sit down here.

Glen. I know that we cannot see the North Star, Melinda, and I fear we've lost our way. But, see! the clouds are passing away, and it'll soon be clear. See! yonder is a star; yonder is another and another. Ah! yonder is the North Star, and we are safe!

"Star of the North! though night winds drift
        The fleecy drapery of the sky
Between thy lamp and me, I lift,
        Yea, lift with hope my sleepless eye,
To the blue heights wherein thou dwellest,
And of a land of freedom tellest.

"Star of the North! while blazing day
        Pours round me its full tide of light,
And hides thy pale but faithful ray,
        I, too, lie hid, and long for night:
For night: I dare not walk at noon,
Nor dare I trust the faithless moon—

"Nor faithless man, whose burning lust
>For gold hath riveted my chain,—
Nor other leader can I trust
>But thee, of even the starry train;
For all the host around thee burning,
Like faithless man, keep turning, turning.

"I may not follow where they go:—
>Star of the North! I look to thee
While on I press; for well I know,
>Thy light and truth shall set me free:—
Thy light, that no poor slave deceiveth;
Thy truth, that all my soul believeth.

"Thy beam is on the glassy breast
>Of the still spring, upon whose brink
I lay my weary limbs to rest,
>And bow my parching lips to drink.
Guide of the friendless negro's way,
I bless thee for this quiet ray!

"In the dark top of southern pines
>I nestled, when the Driver's horn
Called to the field, in lengthening lines,
>My fellows, at the break of morn.
And there I lay till thy sweet face
Looked in upon "my hiding place."

The tangled cane-brake, where I crept
>For shelter from the heat of noon,
And where, while others toiled, I slept,
>Till wakened by the rising moon,
As its stalks felt the night wind free,
Gave me to catch a glimpse of thee.

"Star of the North! in bright array
       The constellations round thee sweep,
Each holding on its nightly way,
       Rising, or sinking in the deep,
And, as it hangs in mid heaven flaming,
The homage of some nation claiming.

"*This* nation to the Eagle cowers;
       Fit ensign! she's a bird of spoil:—
Like worships like! for each devours
       The earnings of another's toil.
I've felt her talons and her beak,
And now the gentler Lion seek.

"The Lion, at the Monarch's feet
       Crouches, and lays his mighty paw
Into her lap!—an emblem meet
       Of England's Queen, and English law:
Queen, that hath made her Islands free!
Law, that holds out its shield to me!

Star of the North! upon that shield
       Thou shinest,—Oh, for ever shine!
The negro, from the cotton field
       Shall, then, beneath its orb recline,
And feed the Lion, couched before it,
Nor heed the Eagle, screaming o'er it!"

With the thoughts of servitude behind us, and the North Star before us, we will go forward with cheerful hearts. Come, Melinda, let's go on.

                                         [*Exit,* L.

Scene 3.—A STREET.

Enter MR. WHITE, R.

Mr. White. I am glad to be once more in a free State. If I am caught again south of Mason and Dixon's line, I'll give them leave to lynch me. I came near losing my life. This is the way our constitutional rights are trampled upon. But what care these men about Constitutions, or any thing else that does not suit them? But I must hasten on.

[*Exit,* L.

Enter CATO, *in disguise,* R.

Cato. I wonder ef dis is me? By golly, I is free as a frog. But maybe I is mistaken; maybe dis ain't me. Cato, is dis you? Yes, seer. Well, now it is me, an' I em a free man. But, stop! I muss change my name, kase ole massa might foller me, and somebody might tell him dat dey seed Cato; so I'll change my name, and den he won't know me ef he sees me. Now, what shall I call myself? I'm now in a suspectable part of de country, an' I muss have a suspectable name. Ah! I'll call myself Alexander Washington Napoleon Pompey Cæsar. Dar, now, dat's a good long, suspectable name, and every body will suspect me. Let me see; I wonder ef I can't make up a song on my escape? I'll try.

AIR— *"Dearest Mae."*

Now, freemen, listen to my song, a story I'll relate,
It happened in de valley of de ole Kentucky State:
Dey marched me out into de fiel', at every break of day,
And work me dar till late sunset, widout a cent of pay.

  Chorus.—Dey work me all de day,
    Widout a bit of pay,
    And thought, because dey fed me well,
    I would not run away.

Massa gave me his ole coat, an' thought I'd happy be,
But I had my eye on de North Star, an' thought of liberty;
Ole massa lock de door, an' den he went to sleep,
I dress myself in his bess clothes, an' jump into de street.

Chorus.—Dey work me all de day,

Widout a bit of pay,

So I took my flight, in the middle of de night,

When de sun was gone away.

Sed I, dis chile's a freeman now, he'll be a slave no more;

I travell'd faster all dat night, dan I ever did before.

I came up to a farmer's house, jest at de break of day,

And saw a white man standin' dar, sed he, "You are a runaway."

Chorus.—Dey work me all de day, &c.

I tole him I had left de whip, an' bayin' of de hound,

To find a place where man is man, ef sich dar can be found;

Dat I had heard, in Canada, dat all mankind are free,

An' dat I was going dar in search of liberty.

Chorus.—Dey work me all de day, &c.

I've not committed any crime, why should I run away?

Oh! shame upon your laws, dat drive me off to Canada.

You loudly boast of liberty, an' say your State is free,

But ef I tarry in your midst, will you protect me?

Chorus.—Dey work me all de day, &c.

[*Exit,* L.

Scene 4.—DINING-ROOM.—TABLE SPREAD.

MRS. NEAL *and* CHARLOTTE.

Mrs. Neal. Thee may put the tea to draw, Charlotte. Thy father will be in soon, and we must have breakfast.

Enter MR. NEAL, L.

I think, Simeon, it is time those people were called. Thee knows that they may be pursued, and we ought not to detain them long here.

Mr. Neal. Yes, Ruth, thou art right. Go, Charlotte, and knock on their chamber door, and tell them that breakfast is ready.

[*Exit* CHARLOTTE, R.

Mrs. N. Poor creatures! I hope they'll reach Canada in safety. They seem to be worthy persons.

Enter CHARLOTTE, R.

Charlotte. I've called them, mother, and they'll soon be down. I'll put the breakfast on the table.

Enter NEIGHBOR JONES, L.

Mr. N. Good morning, James. Thee has heard, I presume, that we have two very interesting persons in the house?

Jones. Yes, I heard that you had two fugitives by the Underground road, last night; and I've come over to fight for them, if any persons come to take them back.

Enter THOMAS, R.

Mr. N. Go, Thomas, and harness up the horses and put them to the covered wagon, and be ready to take these people on, as soon as they get their breakfast. Go, Thomas, and hurry thyself.

[*Exit* THOMAS, R.

And so thee wants to fight, this morning, James?

Jones. Yes; as you belongs to a society that don't believe in fighting, and I does believe in that sort of thing, I thought I'd come and relieve you of that work, if there is any to be done.

Enter GLEN *and* MELINDA, R.

Mr. N. Good morning, friends. I hope thee rested well, last night.

Mrs. N. Yes, I hope thee had a good night's rest.

Glen. I thank you, madam, we did.

Mr. N. I'll introduce thee to our neighbor, James Jones. He's a staunch friend of thy people.

Jones. I am glad to see you. I've come over to render assistance, if any is needed.

Mrs. N. Come, friends, take seats at the table. Thee'll take seats there. [*To* GLEN *and* MELINDA.] [*All take seats at the table.*] Does thee take sugar and milk in thy tea?

Melinda. I thank you, we do.

Jones. I'll look at your *Tribune,* Uncle Simeon, while you're eating.

Mr. N. Thee'll find it on the table.

Mrs. N. I presume thee's anxious to get to thy journey's end?

Glen. Yes, madam, we are. I am told that we are not safe in any of the free States.

Mr. N. I am sorry to tell thee, that that is too true. Thee will not be safe until thee gets on British soil. I wonder what keeps Thomas; he should have been here with the team.

Enter THOMAS, L.

Thomas. All's ready; and I've written the prettiest song that was ever sung. I call it "The Underground Railroad."

Mr. N. Thomas, thee can eat thy breakfast far better than thee can write a song, as thee calls it. Thee must hurry thyself, when I send thee for the horses, Thomas. Here lately, thee takes thy time.

Thomas. Well, you see I've been writing poetry; that's the reason I've been so long. If you wish it, I'll sing it to you.

Jones. Do let us hear the song.

Mrs. Neal. Yes, if Thomas has written a ditty, do let us hear it.

Mr. Neal. Well, Thomas, if thee has a ditty, thee may recite it to us.

Thomas. Well, I'll give it to you. Remember that I call it, "The Underground Railroad."

AIR—*"Wait for the Wagon."*

Oh, where is the invention

    Of this growing age,

Claiming the attention

    Of statesman, priest, or sage,

In the many railways

    Through the nation found,

Equal to the Yankees'

    Railway under-ground?

Chorus.—No one hears the whistle,

    Or rolling of the cars,

    While negroes ride to freedom

    Beyond the stripes and stars.

On the Southern borders
> Are the Railway stations,
Negroes get free orders
> While on the plantations;
For all, of ev'ry color,
> First-class cars are found,
While they ride to freedom
> By Railway under-ground.

> *Chorus.*—No one hears the whistle, &c.

Masters in the morning
> Furiously rage,
Cursing the inventions
> Of this knowing age;
Order out the bloodhounds,
> Swear they'll bring them back,
Dogs return exhausted,
> Cannot find the track.

> *Chorus.*—No one hears the whistle, &c.

Travel is increasing,
> Build a double track,
Cars and engines wanted,
> They'll come, we have no lack.
Clear the track of loafers,
> See that crowded car!
Thousands passing yearly,
> Stock is more than par.

> *Chorus.*—No one hears the whistle, &c.

Jones. Well done! That's a good song. I'd like to have a copy of them verses. [*Knock at the door. Charlotte goes to the door, and returns.*

Enter CATO, L., *still in disguise.*

Mr. Neal. Who is this we have? Another of the outcasts, I presume?

Cato. Yes, seer; I is gwine to Canada, an' I met a man, an' he tole me dat you would give me some wittals an' help me on de way. By golly! ef dar ain't Glen an' Melinda. Dey do n't know me in dese fine clothes. [*Goes up to them.*] Ah, chillen! I is one wid you. I golly, I is here too! [*They shake hands.*]

Glen. Why, it is Cato, as I live!

Melinda. Oh, Cato, I am so glad to see you! But how did you get here?

Cato. Ah, chile, I come wid ole massa to hunt you; an' you see I get tired huntin' you, an' I am now huntin' for Canada. I leff de ole boss in de bed at de hotel; an' you see I thought, afore I left massa, I'd jess change clothes wid him; so, you see, I is fixed up, —ha, ha, ha. Ah, chillen! I is gwine wid you.

Mrs. Neal. Come, sit thee down, and have some breakfast.

Cato. Tank you, madam, I'll do dat. [*Sits down and eats.*

Mr. Neal. This is pleasant for thee to meet one of thy friends.

Glen. Yes, sir, it is; I would be glad if we could meet more of them. I have a mother and sister still in slavery, and I would give worlds, if I possessed them, if by so doing I could release them from their bondage.

Thomas. We are all ready, sir, and the wagon is waiting.

Mrs. Neal. Yes, thee had better start.

Cato. Ef any body tries to take me back to ole massa, I'll pull ebry toof out of dar heads, dat I will! As soon as I get to Canada, I'll set up a doctor shop, an' won't I be poplar? Den I rec'on I will. I'll pull teef fer all de people in Canada. Oh, how I wish I had Hannah wid me! It makes me feel bad when I tink I ain't a-gwine to see my wife no more. But, come, chillen, let's be makin' tracks. Dey say we is most to de British side.

Mr. Neal. Yes, a few miles further, and you'll be safe beyond the reach of the Fugitive-Slave Law.

Cato. Ah, dat's de talk fer dis chile.

[*Exit,* M.D.

Scene 5.—THE NIAGARA RIVER—A FERRY.

FERRYMAN, *fastening his small boat.*

Ferryman, [*advancing, takes out his watch.*] I swan, if it ain't one o'clock. I thought it was dinner time. Now there's no one here, I'll go to dinner, and if any body comes, they can wait until I return. I'll go at once.

[*Exit,* L.

Enter MR. WHITE, R., *with an umbrella.*

Mr. White. I wonder where that ferryman is? I want to cross to Canada. It seems a little showery, or else the mist from the Falls is growing thicker. [*Takes out his sketch-book and pencils,—sketches.*

Enter CANE PEDLAR, R.

Pedlar. Want a good cane to-day, sir? Here's one from Goat Island,— very good, sir,—straight and neat,—only one dollar. I've a wife and nine small children,—youngest is nursing, and the oldest only three years old. Here's a cane from Table Rock, sir. Please buy one! I've had no breakfast to-day. My wife's got the rheumatics, and the children's got the measles. Come, sir, do buy a cane! I've a lame shoulder, and can't work.

Mr. White. Will you stop your confounded talk, and let me alone? Don't you see that I am sketching? You've spoiled a beautiful scene for me, with your nonsense.

Enter 2d PEDLAR, R.

2d Pedlar. Want any bead bags, or money purses? These are all real Ingen bags, made by the Black Hawk Ingens. Here's a pretty bag, sir, only 75 cents. Here's a money purse, 50 cents. Please, sir, buy something! My wife's got the fever and ague, and the house is full of children, and they're all sick. Come, sir, do help a worthy man!

Mr. White. Will you hold your tongue? You've spoiled some of the finest pictures in the world. Don't you see that I am sketching?

[*Exit* PEDLARS, R., *grumbling.*

I am glad those fellows have gone; now I'll go a little further up the shore, and see if I can find another boat. I want to get over.

[*Exit,* L.

Enter DR. GAINES, SCRAGG, *and an* OFFICER.

Officer. I do n't think that your slaves have crossed yet, and my officers will watch the shore below here, while we stroll up the river. If I once get my hands on them, all the Abolitionists in the State shall not take them from me.

Dr. G. I hope they have not got over, for I would not lose them for two thousand dollars, especially the gal.

Enter 1st PEDLAR.

Pedlar. Wish to get a good cane, sir? This stick was cut on the very spot where Sam Patch jumped over the falls. Only fifty cents. I have a sick wife and thirteen children. Please buy a cane; I ain't had no dinner.

Officer. Get out of the way! Gentlemen, we'll go up the shore.

[*Exit,* L.

Enter CATO, R.

Cato. I is loss fum de cumpny, but dis is de ferry, and I spec dey'll soon come. But did n't we have a good time las' night in Buffalo? Dem dar Buffalo gals make my heart flutter, dat dey did. But, tanks be to de Lord, I is got religion. I got it las' night in de meetin'. Before I got religion, I was a great sinner; I got drunk, an' took de name of de Lord in vain. But now I is a conwerted man; I is bound for hebben; I toats de witness in my bosom; I feel dat my name is rote in de book of life. But dem niggers in de Vine Street Church las' night shout an' make sich a fuss, dey give me de headache. But, tank de Lord, I is got religion, an' now I'll be a preacher, and den dey'll call me de Rev. Alexander Washinton Napoleon Pompey Cæsar. Now I'll preach and pull teef, bofe at de same time. Oh, how I wish I had Hannah wid me! Cuss ole massa, fer ef it warn't for him, I could have my wife wid me. Ef I had n't religion, I'd say "Damn ole massa!" but as I is a religious man, an' belongs to de church, I won't say no sich a thing. But who is dat I see comin'? Oh, it's a whole heap of people. Good Lord! what is de matter?

Enter GLEN *and* MELINDA, L., *followed by* OFFICERS.

Glen. Let them come; I am ready for them. He that lays hands on me or my wife shall feel the weight of this club.

Melinda. Oh, Glen, let's die here, rather than again go into slavery.

Officer. I am the United States Marshal. I have a warrant from the Commissioner to take you, and bring you before him. I command assistance.

Enter DR. GAINES, SCRAGG, *and* OFFICER, R.

Dr. Gaines. Here they are. Down with the villain! down with him! but do n't hurt the gal!

Enter MR. WHITE, R.

Mr. White. Why, bless me! these are the slaveholding fellows. I'll fight for freedom! [*Takes hold of his umbrella with both hands.—The fight commences, in which* GLEN, CATO, DR. GAINES, SCRAGG, WHITE, *and the* OFFICERS, *take part.—*FERRYMAN *enters, and runs to his boat.—* DR. GAINES, SCRAGG *and the* OFFICERS *are knocked down,* GLEN, MELINDA *and* CATO *jump into the boat, and as it leaves the shore and floats away,* GLEN *and* CATO *wave their hats, and shout loudly for freedom.—Curtain falls.*

THE END.

OPINIONS OF THE PRESS.

☞ The following are but few of the favorable notices given of "THE ESCAPE," where it has been publicly read:

A novel Dramatic Reading took place last evening at Sansom Street Hall, by WM. WELLS BROWN, the colored dramatic writer, which was highly entertaining, and gave the greatest satisfaction to an intelligent and appreciative audience. The Drama is instructive, as well as very laughable.—*Philadelphia Evening Bulletin.*

All who heard MR. BROWN'S Drama were highly gratified. It is well executed, and was finely delivered.—*Philadelphia Morning Times.*

The Dramatic Reading of Mr. WM. WELLS BROWN, last evening, was well attended, and gave the most unbounded satisfaction. MR. BROWN's Drama is, in itself, a masterly refutation of all apologies for slavery, and abounds in wit, satire, philosophy, argument and facts, all ingeniously interwoven into one of the most interesting dramatic compositions of modern times.—*Auburn (N.Y.) Daily Advertiser.*

MR. BROWN exhibits a dramatic talent possessed by few who have, under the best instructions, made themselves famous on the stage. He evinces a talent for tragic and comic representation rarely combined. If you want a good laugh, go and hear him. If you want instruction or information upon the most interesting question of the day, go and hear him. You cannot fail to be pleased. So highly pleased were those who heard it in Auburn, that twenty-eight of the leading men of the city, over their own signatures, extended an invitation to him, through the *Daily Advertiser,* to return and repeat the Drama. Among them we recognize the names of Hon. B. F. Hall, of the State Senate, and the Rev. Wm. Hosmer, editor of the *Northern Independent.* Such a compliment entitles MR. BROWN to crowded houses wherever he goes.—*Seneca Falls Courier.*

SUGGESTIONS FOR FURTHER READING

WORKS BY WILLIAM WELLS BROWN

The American Fugitive in Europe: Sketches of Places and People Abroad.
Boston: John P. Jewett, 1855.

The Anti-Slavery Harp: A Collection of Songs for Anti-Slavery Meetings.
Boston: Bela Marsh, 1848.

The Black Man, His Antecedents, His Genius, and His Achievements. New
York: Thomas Hamilton, 1863.

*Clotel; Or, The President's Daughter. A Narrative of Slave Life in the United
States.* London: Partridge and Oakey, 1853.

Clotelle: A Tale of the Southern States. Boston: James Redpath Publishers,
1864.

Clotelle; or, The Colored Heroine. A Tale of the Southern States. Boston:
Lee and Shephard, 1867.

*A Description of William Wells Brown's Original Panoramic Views of the
Scenes in the Life of an American Slave, from His Birth in Slavery
to His Death or His Escape to His First Home of Freedom on British
Soil.* London: Charles Gilpin, 1850.

The Escape; or, A Leap for Freedom. A Drama in Five Acts. Boston: R. F.
Walcutt, 1858.

*A Lecture Delivered Before the Female Anti-Slavery Society of Salem,
[Massachusetts,] at Lyceum Hall, Nov. 14, 1847.* Boston: Massachusetts Anti-Slavery Society, 1847.

*Memoir of William Wells Brown, an American Bondman, Written by Him-
self.* Boston: Boston Anti-Slavery Office, 1859.

My Southern Home: Or, The South and Its People. Boston: A. G. Brown,
1880.

Narrative of William W. Brown, a Fugitive Slave. Written by Himself.
Boston: American Anti-Slavery Society, 1847.

The Negro in the American Rebellion: His Heroism and His Fidelity.
   Boston: Lee and Shephard, 1867.
*The Rising Son; or, The Antecedents and Advancement of the Colored
   Race.* Boston: A. G. Brown and Company, 1874.
St. Domingo: Its Revolutions and Its Patriots. A Lecture. Boston: Bela
   Marsh, 1855.
Three Years in Europe; or, Places I Have Seen and People I Have Met.
   London: Charles Gilpin, 1852.

ON THE LIFE AND WRITINGS OF
WILLIAM WELLS BROWN

Andrews, William L. *To Tell a Free Story: The First Century of Afro-American
   Autobiography, 1760–1865.* Urbana: Univ. of Illinois Press, 1986.
[Brown, Josephine]. *Biography of an American Bondman, by His Daugh-
   ter.* 1856. In *Two Biographies by African-American Women*, ed.
   William L. Andrews. New York: Oxford Univ. Press, 1991.
Ellison, Curtis W. *William Wells Brown and Martin R. Delany: A Refer-
   ence Guide.* Boston: G. K. Hall, 1976.
Ernest, John. *Resistance and Reformation in Nineteenth-Century African-
   American Literature: Brown, Wilson, Jacobs, Delany, Douglass, and
   Harper.* Jackson: Univ. Press of Mississippi, 1995.
Farrison, William Edward. *William Wells Brown: Author and Reformer.*
   Chicago: Univ. of Chicago Press, 1969.
Foster, Frances Smith. *Witnessing Slavery: The Development of Antebellum
   Slave Narratives.* 1979. 2d ed. Madison: Univ. of Wisconsin Press,
   1994.
Gilmore, Paul. "'De Genewine Artekil': William Wells Brown, Blackface
   Minstrelsy, and Abolitionism." *American Literature* 69, no. 4 (1997):
   743–80.
Jackson, Blyden. *A History of Afro-American Literature.* Vol. 1. *The Long
   Beginning, 1746–1895.* Baton Rouge: Louisiana State Univ. Press,
   1989.
Loggins, Vernon. *The Negro Author: His Development in America.* New
   York: Columbia Univ. Press, 1931.
Redding, J. Saunders. *To Make a Poet Black.* 1939. Rpt. Ithaca, New York:
   Cornell Univ. Press, 1988.
Robinson, Lisa Clayton. "Brown, William Wells." In *Africana: The
   Encyclopedia of African and African American Experience*, ed.
   Kwame Anthony Appiah and Henry Louis Gates Jr., p. 323. New
   York: Basic Civitas Books, 1999.

Yellin, Jean Fagan. *The Intricate Knot: Black Figures in American Literature, 1776–1863*. New York: New York Univ. Press, 1972.

Zafar, Rafia. *We Wear the Mask: African Americans Write American Literature, 1760–1870*. New York: Columbia Univ. Press, 1997.

ON DRAMA AND BLACKFACE MINSTRELSY

Abramson, Doris E. *Negro Playwrights in the American Theatre, 1925–1959*. New York: Columbia Univ. Press, 1969.

Bean, Annemarie; James V. Hatch; and Brooks McNamara. *Inside the Minstrel Mask: Readings in Nineteenth-Century Blackface Minstrelsy*. Hanover, New Hampshire: Wesleyan Univ. Press, 1996.

Grimsted, David. *Melodrama Unveiled: American Theater and Culture, 1800–1850*. 1968. Rpt. Berkeley: Univ. of California Press, 1987.

Hay, Samuel A. *African American Theatre: A Historical and Critical Analysis*. Cambridge, England: Cambridge Univ. Press, 1994.

Levine, Lawrence W. *Highbrow/Lowbrow: The Emergence of Cultural Hierarchy in America*. Cambridge, Massachusetts: Harvard Univ. Press, 1988.

Lhamon, W. T., Jr. *Raising Cain: Blackface Performance from Jim Crow to Hip Hop*. Cambridge, Massachusetts: Harvard Univ. Press, 1998.

Lott, Eric. *Love and Theft: Blackface Minstrelsy and the American Working Class*. New York: Oxford Univ. Press, 1993.

Mitchell, Loften. *Voices of the Black Theatre*. Clifton, New Jersey: James T. White and Company, 1975.

Nathan, Hans. *Dan Emmett and the Rise of Early Negro Minstrelsy*. Norman: Univ. of Oklahoma Press, 1962.

Peterson, Bernard L., Jr. *Early Black American Playwrights and Dramatic Writers: A Biographical Directory and Catalog of Plays, Films, and Broadcasting Scripts*. New York: Greenwood Press, 1990.

Toll, Robert C. *Blacking Up: The Minstrel Show in Nineteenth-Century America*. New York: Oxford Univ. Press, 1974.

Wittke, Carl. *Tambo and Bones: A History of the American Minstrel Stage*. New York: Greenwood Press, 1968.

ON RACE IN THE UNITED STATES

Berzon, Judith R. *Neither White Nor Black: The Mulatto Character in American Fiction*. New York: New York Univ. Press, 1978.

Cassuto, Leonard. *The Inhuman Race: The Racial Grotesque in American Literature and Culture*. New York: Columbia Univ. Press, 1997.

Davis, F. James. *Who Is Black? One Nation's Definition.* University Park: Pennsylvania State Univ. Press, 1992.

Fredrickson, George M. *The Black Image in the White Mind: The Debate on Afro-American Character and Destiny, 1817–1914.* New York: Harper, 1971.

Goldberg, David Theo. *Racist Culture: Philosophy and the Politics of Meaning.* Cambridge, Massachusetts: Blackwell, 1993.

Gossett, Thomas F. *Race: The History of an Idea in America.* 1963. Rpt. New York: Schocken Books, 1965.

Horsman, Reginald. *Race and Manifest Destiny: The Origins of American Racial Anglo-Saxonism.* Cambridge, Massachusetts: Harvard Univ. Press, 1981.

Nelson, Dana. *National Manhood: Capitalist Citizenship and the Imagined Fraternity of White Men.* Durham, N.C.: Duke Univ. Press, 1998.

Roediger, David R. *The Wages of Whiteness: Race and the Making of the American Working Class.* London: Verso, 1991.

Saxton, Alexander. *The Rise and Fall of the White Republic: Class Politics and Mass Culture in Nineteenth-Century America.* London: Verso, 1990.

Smith, Rogers M. *Civic Ideals: Conflicting Visions of Citizenship in U.S. History.* New Haven, Connecticut: Yale Univ. Press, 1997.

Sollors, Werner. *Neither Black Nor White Yet Both: Thematic Explorations of Interracial Literature.* New York: Oxford Univ. Press, 1997.

Santon, William. *The Leopard's Spots: Scientific Attitudes Toward Race in America, 1815–1859.* 1960. Rpt. Chicago: Univ. of Chicago Press, 1982.

Takaki, Ronald. *Iron Cages: Race and Culture in Nineteenth-Century America.* New York: Oxford Univ. Press, 1990.

Van Deburg, William L. *Slavery and Race in American Popular Culture.* Madison: Univ. of Wisconsin Press, 1984.

Weigman, Robyn. *American Anatomies: Theorizing Race and Gender.* Durham, North Carolina: Duke Univ. Press, 1995.

Williamson, Joel. *New People: Miscegenation and Mulattoes in the United States.* Baton Rouge: Louisiana State Univ. Press, 1995.

ON SLAVERY AND ANTISLAVERY MOVEMENTS

Bender, Thomas, ed. *The Antislavery Debate: Capitalism and Abolitionism as a Problem in Historical Interpretation.* Berkeley: Univ. of California Press, 1992.

Castronovo, Russ. *Fathering the Nation: American Genealogies of Slavery and Freedom.* Berkeley: Univ. of California Press, 1995.

Davis, David Brion. *The Slave Power Conspiracy and the Paranoid Style.* Baton Rouge: Louisiana State Univ. Press, 1969.

Frey, Sylvia R. *Water from the Rock: Black Resistance in a Revolutionary Age.* Princeton, New Jersey: Princeton Univ. Press, 1991.

Gara, Larry. *The Liberty Line: The Legend of the Underground Railroad.* Lexington: Univ. of Kentucky Press, 1961.

Genovese, Eugene D. *From Rebellion to Revolution: Afro-American Slave Revolts in the Making of the Modern World.* Baton Rouge: Louisiana State Univ. Press, 1979.

———. *Roll, Jordan, Roll: The World the Slaves Made.* New York: Vintage, 1976.

Gerteis, Louis S. *Morality and Utility in American Antislavery Reform.* Chapel Hill. Univ. of North Carolina Press, 1987.

Gutman, Herbert G. *The Black Family in Slavery and Freedom, 1750–1925.* New York: Vintage, 1977.

Harrold, Stanley. *The Abolitionists and the South, 1831–1861.* Lexington: Univ. of Kentucky Press, 1995.

Horton, James Oliver. *Free People of Color: Inside the African American Community.* Washington, D.C.: Smithsonian Institution Press, 1993.

Jones, Jacqueline. *Labor of Love, Labor of Sorrow: Black Women, Work, and the Family, from Slavery to the Present.* 1985. New York: Vintage Books, 1986.

Kaufman, Allen. *Capitalism, Slavery, and Republican Values: Antebellum Political Economists, 1819–1848.* Austin: Univ. of Texas Press, 1982.

Kraditor, Aileen S. *Means and Ends in American Abolitionism: Garrison and His Critics in Strategy and Tactics, 1834–1850.* New York: Vintage, 1970.

Levine, Lawrence W. *Black Culture and Black Consciousness: Afro-American Folk Thought from Slavery to Freedom.* New York: Oxford Univ. Press, 1977.

Litwack, Leon F. *North of Slavery: The Negro in the Free States, 1790–1860.* Chicago: Phoenix Books, Univ. of Chicago Press, 1961.

Miller, William Lee. *Arguing About Slavery: The Great Battle in the United States Congress.* New York: Knopf, 1996.

Morgan, Edmund. *American Slavery, American Freedom: The Ordeal of Colonial Virginia.* New York: W. W. Norton, 1975.

Oakes, James. *Slavery and Freedom: An Interpretation of the Old South.* New York: Knopf, 1990.

Parish, Peter J. *Slavery: History and Historians.* New York: Harper and Row, 1989.

Patterson, Orlando. *Slavery and Social Death: A Comparative Study.* Cambridge, Massachusetts: Harvard Univ. Press, 1982.

Quarles, Benjamin. *Black Abolitionists*. New York: Oxford Univ. Press, 1969.

Stuckey, Sterling. *Slave Culture: Nationalist Theory and the Foundations of Black America*. New York: Oxford Univ. Press, 1987.

Tise, Larry E. *Proslavery: A History of the Defense of Slavery in America, 1701–1840*. Athens: Univ. of Georgia Press, 1987.

White, Deborah Gray. *Ar'n't I a Woman? Female Slaves in the Plantation South*. New York: W. W. Norton, 1985.

Wilson, Carol. *Freedom at Risk: The Kidnapping of Free Blacks in America, 1780–1865*. Lexington: Univ. Press of Kentucky, 1994.

Yellin, Jean Fagan. *Women and Sisters: The Antislavery Feminists in American Culture*. New Haven, Connecticut: Yale Univ. Press, 1989.

Yellin, Jean Fagan, and John C. Van Horne, eds. *The Abolitionist Sisterhood: Women's Political Culture in Antebellum America*. Ithaca, New York: Cornell Univ. Press, 1994.

On Identity and Social Performance

Butler, Judith. *Bodies That Matter: On the Discursive Limits of "Sex."* New York: Routledge, 1993.

Fernandez, James W. *Persuasions and Performances: The Play of Tropes in Culture*. Bloomington: Indiana Univ. Press, 1986.

Goffman, Erving. *The Presentation of Self in Everyday Life*. New York: Anchor Books, 1959.

Roach, Joseph. *Cities of the Dead: Circum-Atlantic Performance*. New York: Columbia Univ. Press, 1996.

Schechner, Richard. *Between Theater and Anthropology*. Philadelphia: Univ. of Pennsylvania Press, 1985.

———. *The Future of Ritual: Writings on Culture and Performance*. London: Routledge, 1993.

Schechner, Richard, and Willa Appel, eds. *By Means of Performance: Intercultural Studies of Theatre and Ritual*. Cambridge, England: Cambridge Univ. Press, 1990.

Turner, Victor. *From Ritual to Theatre: The Human Seriousness of Play*. New York: Performing Arts Journal Publications, 1982.